almost free

EVA SHEPPARD WOLF

almost free

A STORY ABOUT
FAMILY AND RACE
IN ANTEBELLUM
VIRGINIA

The University of Georgia Press
Athens & London

A Sarah Mills Hodge Fund Publication
This publication is made possible in part through a grant from the Hodge
Foundation in memory of its founder, Sarah Mills Hodge, who devoted her life
to the relief and education of African Americans in Savannah, Georgia.

Designed by Walton Harris
Set in 10.5 / 14 Adobe Caslon Pro
Printed and bound by Thomson-Shore
The paper in this book meets the guidelines for permanence
and durability of the Committee on Production Guidelines
for Book Longevity of the Council on Library Resources.
Printed in the United States of America

16 15 14 13 12 P 5 4 3 2 1

Library of Congress Cataloging-in-Publication Data

Wolf, Eva Sheppard, 1969–
Almost free : a story about family and race in antebellum Virginia / Eva
Sheppard Wolf.
	p.	cm. — (Race in the Atlantic world, 1700–1900)
Includes bibliographical references and index.
ISBN-13: 978-0-8203-3229-1 (hardcover : alk. paper)
ISBN-10: 0-8203-3229-1 (hardcover : alk. paper)
ISBN-13: 978-0-8203-3230-7 (pbk. : alk. paper)
ISBN-10: 0-8203-3230-5 (pbk. : alk. paper)
1. Johnson, Samuel, 1775?–1842. 2. Freedmen—Virginia—Fauquier County—
Biography. 3. African Americans—Legal status, laws, etc.—Virginia—
History—19th century. 4. African American families—Virginia—Fauquier
County—Social conditions—19th century. 5. Slaves—Emancipation—
Virginia—Fauquier County—History—19th century. 6. Fauquier County
(Va.)—Race relations—History—19th century. 7. Fauquier County
(Va.)—Social conditions—19th century. I. Title.
F232.F3W65 2012
975.5'03092—dc23
[B]	2011044234

British Library Cataloging-in-Publication Data available

To the men, big and little, who make my family —
Sven, Matthew, Ezra — with my deepest love

CONTENTS

ILLUSTRATIONS

AUTHOR'S NOTE

THIS BOOK IS NOT FICTION. I have not made up facts, moved events around in time, or invented dialogue. But this book, even more than most history books, is an act of imagination. I wanted to bring to life a person who reached out to me across the years and through the documents. Because those documents are spare and relatively few, I have had to fill in the gaps with my knowledge of antebellum Virginia and human behavior. I have endeavored to indicate clearly what I know for certain and what I have inferred, although I have tried to avoid an abundance of conditional phrases. I trust the reader will employ her or his critical abilities to see the instances where I could have interpreted evidence differently but did not.

It has been a personal journey to write the story of Samuel Johnson. I hope that for readers too the journey becomes a personal one, and that Samuel Johnson—obscure and long dead—enters their hearts as he has entered mine, and takes his rightful place in the grand American story.

almost free

CHAPTER ONE

a new birth of freedom

SAMUEL JOHNSON STEPPED from the dim courthouse to the bright outdoors, the air heavy with late summer's smells—grass, earth, horses, sweat. The town center stirred with the bustle of court day. Men and women from miles around had come to Warrenton, the Fauquier County seat, to take care of business, to meet, to gossip. Several trials had already been held that day, and some of the participants had gathered in Norris's tavern behind the courthouse. Johnson knew Norris's tavern and many of the people inside it quite well since he had worked there as a slave for more than a decade. Now he was a free man. He had just watched as the county justices ordered that the deed ensuring Johnson's liberty be officially recorded. So before he returned to the tavern to work, Samuel Johnson stood a moment to take in the scene—to see whether he felt different and whether the world had different colors now that he was liberated. He breathed in deeply, closing his eyes, held the breath a moment, and exhaled slowly. Then he opened his eyes and walked toward the tavern.

Or maybe not. Because, like most people who were born as slaves in Virginia, Samuel Johnson could not write, he left no private record of his life—no letters, diaries, or financial account books. We cannot be sure of how he felt about his liberty, or what he saw or smelled, or even whether he attended the proceedings at the courthouse on August 25, 1812, when the deed of manumission that his owner had written three weeks before was filed with the clerk.[1] Maybe he was home, ill with a bad late-summer flu. Or maybe he continued to work at the tavern while the deed's two witnesses, Thomas Moore and tavern owner Thaddeus Norris, went to the courthouse without him to affirm the deed's legitimacy. Without his personal account we simply cannot know for certain how Samuel Johnson behaved on that very important day, although we can guess at likely scenarios based on the records that are available.

There are other, more basic facts that Johnson's birth into slavery have erased: precisely when he was born, where, and to whom; how he got to Fauquier County; why he was chosen to be a servant in the tavern. It is one of slavery's functions to obliterate personhood, to wipe out personal history.

But slaves and free blacks did have personal histories even if most of them are lost to us. Fortunately, Samuel Johnson left behind sufficient public records to reveal the arc of his life as well as some of his deepest thoughts, concerns, and feelings. A careful, close reading of Johnson's documentary imprint—deeds, wills, tax records, court papers, and especially the extraordinary series of petitions that he and his family sent to the state legislature over a nearly thirty-year period from 1811 to 1838—gives a fuller picture of him and his family than we have of almost all contemporaneous free black Virginians. And while any historian would like to have more rather than fewer records, even a large archive, such as the one Thomas Jefferson left behind, can mislead its readers or leave important questions unanswered. Rather than fret over the difficulties of telling Samuel Johnson's story, we will forge ahead, informed by a large body of knowledge that provides crucial context for Johnson's life and experience.

Samuel Johnson's story imparts biographical weight and specificity to our general understanding of how free blacks lived in the era of slavery, but it does more than fill in a chink in our wall of knowledge. In order to understand a society deeply, we must look not only at its center, the majority's experience, but also at the experiences of those on its edges where a society's values and norms are delineated. Free black people constituted a small minority in antebellum Virginia, about 3.1 percent of the state's population in 1810 and about 7.2 percent of Virginia's black population, itself (slaves and free blacks together) more than two-fifths of Virginia's population.[2] Free blacks made up an anomalous population, neither part of the very large slave society nor part of the free white society. Those living on the margins, as Samuel Johnson and other free black people did, helped to define through their experiences and their social interactions precisely what the margins contained between them.

Of particular interest, the story of Samuel Johnson and his family illuminates how race operated in Virginia as something people themselves created and re-created in their multiple interactions with one another. When we examine Johnson's experience in his community of Warrenton, Virginia, we see that race worked differently from what we might expect based on a reading of the laws regarding free people of color or on white Virginians' frequently expressed and strong antipathy toward free blacks. Race in antebellum Virginia was simultaneously momentous and tenuous. We see too that a broad space existed between freedom and slavery—that freedom was not simply slavery's opposite.[3] The world we view, then, is a complex one, and sometimes the scene is blurry, the details fuzzy, and we are left to fill in the picture with imaginings.

So, imagine: From where he stood outside the courthouse, Johnson could see most of the town of Warrenton. The courthouse marked the town's center, and before being incorporated as Warrenton (named after the Revolutionary hero and Massachusetts man Joseph Warren), the town had been called simply Fauquier Court House.[4] With his back to the courthouse, Johnson could look to his right to Main Street with its shops and houses. Where the buildings ended, Main Street ran southeast out of town and became "the road to Fredericksburg," which was approximately forty miles distant. Meeting Main Street in front of him was Court Lane, which ran a couple of blocks northeast before turning to become the road to Alexandria, about fifty miles away. And just to his left, abutting the courthouse, stood the jail (now the Fauquier Historical Society's Old Jail Museum), with lawyers' offices conveniently nearby. If we read backward to 1812 from what we know existed in 1819, we can imagine that he also saw a cabinetmaker's shop, the offices of several doctors, and the shops of the town's hat maker, tanners, and clock maker. With all of these conveniences and with its buildings fairly close together, Warrenton was about as urban as any place in Virginia except for its few real cities, such as Richmond and Alexandria. Warrenton was much more modest and retained a rural flavor; people grew wheat and corn on some of the town lots even up to 1840.[5]

Because Warrenton ran only a few blocks in any direction, if Johnson stood in front of the courthouse, he could have easily seen beyond the town's boundaries to the rolling countryside. Fauquier County lies in Virginia's Piedmont region, situated between the lowlands of the coastal plain and the great Appalachian range. It is beautiful country, gently hilly, often green, fertile. The land had appealed to the wealthy gentlemen of the eastern lowlands, men such as Richard Henry Lee, an indomitable member of the Lee family and, like Joseph Warren, a Revolutionary who, along with others, bought up huge tracts of land in Fauquier as an investment. Lee owned the land that became the county seat, although he never settled there.[6] Like Lee, many of the early investors divided their vast landholdings into smaller plots to sell to settlers. By contrast, the Marshall family, of whom Chief Justice John Marshall would become the most famous member, did settle in Fauquier County, and several family members served as county leaders. In Samuel Johnson's time, the county lay in the orbit of Washington, D.C., as is still true today. The county's farm-

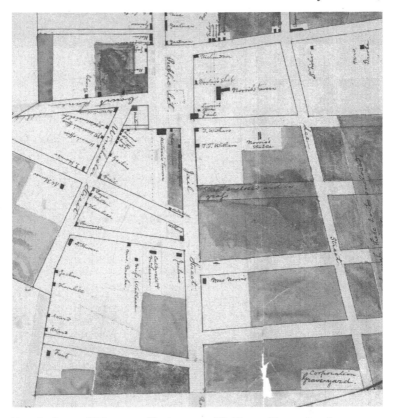

Detail of map of Warrenton, Virginia, 1840. Visible on this map are the un-labeled courthouse on the public lot, Norris's tavern to the right (southwest) of the courthouse, and Mrs. Norris's house on Jail Street. Most of the shaded areas indicate lots with grass, wheat, corn, or oats. Citizens petition, 19 Jan. 1841, Fauquier County, LP.

ers shipped tobacco and surplus wheat and corn to Alexandria, which borders Washington. Some of the produce ended up on the tables of Washington's residents, and some was loaded onto ships and transported beyond the United States. The local newspapers kept track of prices at Alexandria and Fredericksburg for products such as wheat, flour, butter, bacon, and lard.[7]

Even though the kind of farming done in Fauquier differed

significantly from the labor-intensive, staple-crop farming most associated with slavery, Fauquier County contained a significant number of slaves, more than ten thousand in 1810 out of a total population of close to twenty-three thousand people. Even in this Piedmont county outside the plantation region, slaves made up 46 percent of the population, significantly less than in Tidewater counties like Charles City County, where they were nearly 60 percent, but close to the average in Virginia as a whole and much more than in places farther west like Greenbrier County, where less than 10 percent of the population was enslaved.[8] Perhaps Samuel Johnson had relatives who worked as slaves in the fields of the county's wheat and tobacco farms. He was lucky not to be among them since field hands had much less opportunity to gain freedom than did slaves who, like Johnson, worked in public settings or as artisans.

The story of how Samuel Johnson, a self-described "mulatto" man, came to work in one of those public spaces — Norris's tavern — is a story of three continents, a story Johnson literally

Map of Virginia, 1811. Drawn by Mary Lee Eggart.

embodied as an American man of both African and European ancestry. And while the point of this book is to deal as much as possible in specifics, here we must tell a global and rather general tale.

On his mother's side (her name is unknown), the story begins in western Africa, from which almost all American slaves originated. We know that it was his maternal ancestors who were African because according to Virginia law, and American slave law generally, children followed the condition of their mother. If Johnson started out life enslaved, it was because somewhere back in time, one of his mother's people had been enslaved in western Africa. There, in the 1600s and 1700s, lived a complex array of peoples, some organized loosely into villages without any political superstructure, and some belonging to powerful kingdoms with elaborate social structures, wealthy elites, and large armies. The political history of western Africa in this period was fluid, complicated, and often violent, especially after the fifteenth century, when western Africans found that they could sell their war captives to the Europeans who had begun arriving on the coast. Perhaps Samuel Johnson's African ancestor had belonged to a self-contained village that fell victim to invasion by a superior force. Perhaps she had been kidnapped by raiders anxious for profit. Or maybe she had first served as a slave in Africa and was only later sold to European traders. However it happened, it was bad luck to be sold out of Africa instead of being kept among her original captors or owners, as most female and child captives and slaves were. (Captive and enslaved men, it was feared, might join forces and rebel against their captors, so they were often either killed, sometimes ritualistically, or sold away.) She then joined the ten million Africans who, over the course of four centuries, forcibly crossed the Atlantic Ocean in what is called the Middle Passage from their homes in Africa to the Americas.[9]

Samuel Johnson's paternal ancestors probably had a part in making all that happen. If Johnson's mother was of African de-

Fauquier County jailhouse. The brick portion was built in 1808, and the stone addition in 1823. Samuel Johnson would have walked past this building daily. Photo by Eva Sheppard Wolf.

scent and Johnson himself a "mulatto," then his paternal ances-tors came from Europe. As Europeans expanded their power across the Atlantic beginning with Columbus at the end of the fifteenth century, they set up large and profitable plantations in their new world. They imported numerous laborers to grow the products, especially sugar, that Europeans increasingly craved. Virginia was not warm enough for sugar, so planters there grew tobacco, which satisfied another relatively new European craving. Samuel Johnson's father's family likely farmed some tobacco and owned slaves, as did more than half of Virginia families in the mid-eighteenth century. They participated, perhaps unthinkingly, in the brutal production and transportation of African slaves.[10]

And brutal it was. For Samuel Johnson's African ancestor, as for all captive Africans, the passage across the Atlantic from her home to her new life as a plantation slave was torturous. Slaves became commodities in the eyes of those who sold and transported them; turning people into things made it easier to treat them miserably. Slave traders, like other merchants, thought in terms of profit and loss. For them it was cost efficient to ship as many slaves as possible on each voyage, even if that meant that cramped conditions would cause some percentage of their human cargo to die along the way. Maintaining control over unwilling passengers necessitated keeping the men chained together, often packed into holds below deck that were so small that the slaves could not stand up. They lay bound together, forced to urinate and defecate where they lay, and to remain in the filth and stench until sailors cleaned out the hold. Cleaning out the hold usually coincided with the time the male captives were led onto the ship's deck to get some fresh air and a bit of forced jumping about to keep them from becoming too weak and unsalable. On deck the ship's crew fed the slaves enough to keep them alive, usually some form of gruel, a thin bean soup, or yams. Depressed or angry slaves who refused to eat were tortured until they did. Again, it was a matter of profit and loss. Often allowed a bit more mobility than the men, female slaves could on some ships spend much of the day on deck, so Samuel Johnson's ancestor probably found herself better off than many captives in that she could stretch her legs and breathe clean air. Still, the overwhelming experience of the Atlantic voyage was one of horror, which could last a few weeks or close to two months, depending on the wind. For Johnson's ancestor the journey probably took months, since few ships traveled directly between Africa and North America. Instead, many of the slaves arriving in Virginia had first stopped in the Caribbean; Virginia often got the slaves the Caribbean planters did not want.[11]

If Samuel Johnson's African ancestor suffered extremely bad luck first in being captured, and then in being sold to slave traders, she fared better than most African slaves when she arrived in North America, where less than one-twentieth of all slaves landed. Life on a North American plantation was not, of course, what she would have chosen, and she certainly found American slavery to be much harsher and longer lasting than slavery in Africa, where slaves or their children could become true members of the community. But North America's plantations, even the rice plantations of South Carolina, were less deadly to slaves than the sugar plantations of Caribbean islands like Barbados, where hard work and disease made slaves too unwell to sustain their population through natural reproduction. In Virginia, Johnson's African grandmother or great-grandmother probably worked on one of the colony's tobacco farms, like most colonial Virginia slaves. Raising tobacco was tedious and tiring work, requiring careful attention to each individual tobacco plant throughout the growing season. Together, the tobacco laborers had to hoe the ground around the plants, pick off any pests, and pluck extra leaves and buds to produce just a few large tobacco leaves. At harvest time they cut the leaves off the stalks, dried them, and then packed them in barrels for shipment to England. Adding to the difficulty of the work was the terrible homesickness that Johnson's African ancestor must have felt. If she arrived around the turn of the eighteenth century, she probably worked alongside indentured white servants as well as other Africans, though not ones she necessarily shared a language with; if she lived on a small farm, she might have worked alongside the plantation owner himself. If she arrived in the mid-eighteenth century, however, her fellow workers consisted almost entirely of Africans and their descendants.[12]

As unappealing as the work was—one of the reasons white Virginians turned to slave labor in the late seventeenth century—it did not drain Samuel Johnson's ancestor of life. She, like many enslaved women in Virginia, had at least one child. So many enslaved women bore children that by the time of the American Revolution, Virginia-born slaves outnumbered imported slaves. By then, some white Virginians, perhaps Samuel Johnson's father among them, felt that the colony had more slaves than it needed, about two hundred thousand out of a total Virginia population of half a million.[13]

Johnson's mother thus lived as a slave at the time that the whites around her were beginning to declare, in the language of the European Enlightenment, that liberty was a universal right. About the year 1775 or 1776 she brought a son, Samuel, into that enlightened world.[14] He would come to hunger for the same liberty that so many white Virginians, now turned into American Revolutionaries, were willing to fight the king of England for.

Another, much more famous Samuel Johnson—an Englishman—lived at that time, and in a 1775 pamphlet attacking Americans' Revolutionary arguments, he pointedly asked, "How is it that we hear the loudest yelps for liberty among the drivers of negroes?"[15] It made sense that a British critic of the Revolution would perceive a deep conflict between declaring liberty to be a universal right and holding 20 percent of the American population in bondage. But American Revolutionaries saw it too.

In Virginia, though, such a perception could go only so far toward spurring changes in the slave system. Virginia depended on slaves to grow its main export crop, slaves dominated the population in many of the eastern counties, and slaves accounted for 40 percent of the state's population as a whole.[16] Nevertheless, enough change took place that it was possible, though difficult, for the enslaved Samuel Johnson to find liberty. Had Johnson lived farther north, things would have been easier. Where slavery had less economic power, the American Revolution and its ideology of liberty had a greater effect on lessening or ending it. From New Jersey northward the new states of the United States of America passed gradual emancipation laws or outlawed slavery by other means in the years between the Revolution and the early nineteenth century. Pennsylvania was the first, declaring in 1780 that any child born to a slave mother after March 1 of that year would be free after he or she turned twenty-eight years old. Emancipation laws in other states either freed slave children immediately after their births, as in Rhode Island, or provided slightly shorter terms of service than did the Pennsylvania law. New York and New Jersey, the last two northern states to pass emancipation acts, symbolically linked emancipation to the Revolution by setting July 4 as the date after which newly born children would no longer be slaves for life (1799 in New York, 1804 in New Jersey). From Delaware southward, in those states where slavery remained fully legal, Revolutionary leaders nevertheless sought to stem slavery's increase. They did this less from humanitarian motives than for fear of slave rebellion. But Revolutionary-era leaders did perceive the injustice of the slave trade, and all states passed laws barring the further importation of slaves from Africa. Only South Carolina opened up the Atlantic slave trade again, from 1803 to 1807, before a new federal law made the trade illegal.[17]

Virginia's leaders, like those in Delaware and Maryland, additionally eased restrictions on freeing slaves, an important change that made Samuel Johnson's own emancipation possible. In 1782 the Virginia legislature passed a law that allowed slaveholders to free their slaves and allowed the freed people to remain in the commonwealth. Before then, according to a colonial statute, a slave could only be manumitted, or emancipated, with the express permission of the governor and council (the governor's advisory body), and even then the freed person could not remain in Virginia more than six months unless he or she were granted special permission. With the abolition during the Revolution of the council and its replacement by a state senate, the law needed revision to reflect the new governmental arrangement. In addition, restrictions on slaveholders' actions, including restrictions on manumission, did not comport with the Revolutionaries' emphasis on individuals' control over their property, including the power to free that property. Acting amid persistent Quaker lobbying for a law that would allow them to emancipate their slaves, the legislators wrote a new law that permitted anyone to manumit any healthy adult slave under the age of forty-five by a simple act of a deed or will. Perhaps the most significant aspect of the 1782 law was that it broke from previous practice—and from earlier (failed) manumission bills—by allowing newly freed people to remain in Virginia with their families and communities rather than depart.[18]

Samuel Johnson was only about seven years old when the new manumission law passed, and maybe he knew nothing about it. But given his later perceptiveness and attention to what went on around him, it is likely that even as a small child he became aware that a legal way to escape slavery had opened up. Before that, the only escape seemed to be to run, as thousands of enslaved Virginians had done during the War for Independence. Freedom in Pennsylvania was not far away, and its main city of Philadelphia was becoming a magnet for free blacks, but most Fauquier County slaves did not have the appetite for the risks that running away entailed, nor did they have the desire to leave their families and friends behind. With the 1782 law it was possible both to become free and to remain in one's home.

Perhaps Samuel Johnson wanted freedom especially because as a "mulatto," later described as a "bright mulatto," he knew that his father, and possibly also his maternal grandfather, had been white and therefore free.[19] Although many whites had come to the Americas involuntarily or as indentured servants who during the time of their servitude could not control their destinies, Johnson's European ancestors had never been slaves. Colonial laws always reserved slavery for nonwhites. Having descended in part from free white people must have made Johnson all the more aware of history's vagaries, all the more anxious to earn the freedom that his father's people had had.

That mixed heritage, part slave and part free, was typical among those who became "free negroes." A full three-quarters of the Fauquier County "free negroes" who registered with officials in the 1810s and 1820s were "mulatto" or "light."[20] Being "mulatto" also helps explain *why* many of them became free. Sometimes a white father might arrange for the freedom of his "mulatto" offspring. In addition, white people were more likely to place light-skinned slaves in such positions beyond the field as coopers, smiths, or household workers. They read dark skin as a sign of physical strength and seem to have read light skin as a sign of greater mental capacity.[21] (It could have been different. Whites could have reviled light-skinned blacks as evidence of violence — the rape of enslaved women by white men — or as unnatural mixtures between the two "races.") Skilled slaves who worked closely with whites could more easily gain their freedom than could field workers, who remained distant from their owners and had little access to the cash economy. In Samuel Johnson's case, his "bright" skin and insistent self-definition as a "mulatto" — he took pride in his part-white ancestry — suggest that his white father may have placed Samuel in Norris's tavern as the slave of Edward Digges, Norris's business partner. His light skin made whites more comfortable with him and thus made him a good candidate for a tavern servant. In the tavern, Johnson waited on tables, helped clean, and assisted customers. By 1811 he even oversaw other workers as the tavern's "principal servant."[22]

And he earned tips. Tipping slaves might seem strange if one considers slaves to be owned beings who worked under compulsion and without compensation. But tipping was common and a mark of gentlemanly behavior. George Washington, for example, noted in his financial ledger the tips he gave to Martha Custis's slaves when he visited during their courtship.[23] Johnson was able to tuck away the tips he received and over time build up considerable savings.

Most important about his tavern job was that it put him at the very center of the county's public life. Every month each county in Virginia had its handful of court days, during which the justices assembled so that citizens could take care of such mundane transactions as the filing of deeds or wills, or more contentious business such as civil or criminal suits. Court days gave white Virginians, who often lived at some distance from one another, a chance to come together. But white Virginians did not do their communing in the courthouses themselves; those were places of serious business. Their socializing centered on the taverns that lay nearby. On the other days of the month a tavern's customers typically included the local lawyers and other county officials.[24] In great contrast to field hands, perhaps including his own mother, Johnson earned some cash and worked in a place that gave him access to the most influential people in the county. Indeed, many of the white people who would play major roles in his life were men of wealth and power: trustees of the town, judges on the court, even representatives to the state and national legislatures.

Picking up bits of conversation as he went about his tavern work, Samuel Johnson probably heard of some lucky slaves who had been liberated because their masters, influenced by a combination of Revolutionary ideals and religious imperatives to do justice, freed all their bondspeople. But there were no local examples of large-scale acts of manumission, such as when Robert Carter famously freed 450 slaves. Fauquier County was overrun neither with idealistic slaveholders willing to part with their property to live out Revolutionary principles nor with religious radicals dedicated to earthly justice. But in the courthouse near the tavern, slaveowners recorded acts of manumission that Johnson could take as a source of inspiration. He likely knew of Moll, whose husband purchased her in 1792 and presumably freed her. Or of Fanny Davis, who purchased herself from her owner in 1800 for forty pounds. Or of Judy Patience, who lived in Warrenton and who had been freed by her owner that same year.[25]

It was around then, in 1800, when he was in his mid-twenties, that Johnson determined that he too could become free. Unlike Judy Patience's owner, Johnson's owner, Edward Digges, did not consider freeing Johnson without compensation, no matter how much affection he might have had for his slave. Digges was a law-and-order man, a sheriff in 1795, and an officer of the county court beginning that year. He was also an entrepreneurial type. His business ventures included a mill as well as the tavern. Digges needed workers for his various ventures, and besides Samuel Johnson he owned about a dozen slaves, none of whom he freed.[26]

Johnson would have to earn his freedom; he would have to purchase it as Fanny Davis had done. But even that was not assured. Nothing required Digges to allow Johnson to purchase himself even if he raised a large amount of money. In addition, since slaves did not have legal personhood and could not legally marry, own property, enter into contracts, or make wills, any agreement forged between Johnson and Digges lacked legal validity. Johnson could not sue if Digges were to renege. He would have to convince Digges to allow him to purchase himself and then would have to trust Digges to carry out his end of the bargain.

As Johnson was contemplating these things, something happened that probably made him even more anxious and determined to come to an understanding with Digges. In the late summer of 1800, news broke of a massive and sophisticated plan by slaves in the Richmond area to rebel. The newspapers downplayed the seriousness of the scheme, one calling the plot a "shallow" one that would have been easily put down.[27] At the same time, though, they revealed the fear that the news had generated, noting that the "public mind has been much involved in dangerous apprehensions" and that the "alarm is awful in Virginia and South Carolina."[28] During the trials of the would-be rebels, details of the plan came out. Gabriel, the leader, expected that after the rebels had taken the capitol in Richmond, "if the white people agreed to their freedom they would then hoist a white flag, and [Gabriel] would dine and drink with the merchants of the city." Gabriel, in other words, wanted to use the uprising as a bargaining chip, a way to extract freedom for himself and all other slaves. He even expected poor whites to join him; had apparently enlisted two Frenchmen in the plot; and had declared that no

Quakers, Methodists, or Frenchmen were to be harmed during the insurrection, because he viewed those groups as advocates of freedom. In his mind he was fighting the same battle fought by the Americans in the 1770s. The flag he intended to carry on the night of the rebellion was to read, echoing Patrick Henry, "death or Liberty."[29]

In conjunction with two more conspiracies discovered in 1802, Gabriel's Rebellion (though it never took place) helped spark a backlash against some of the more liberal policies of the Revolutionary era, including the 1782 manumission law. One newspaper writer blamed the plot on the ideology of the Revolution, singling out Thomas Jefferson, author of the Declaration of Independence, for condemnation: "For every outrage and murder the Negroes may commit, you [Jefferson] stand accountable."[30]

In Norris's tavern Samuel Johnson no doubt overheard some of this talk and understood that Gabriel's plot made many white Virginians jittery about granting their slaves any liberties. If Johnson were going to talk to Digges about buying his freedom, he had to do it soon.

And so he did. Johnson and Digges came to an agreement in 1802 but not without the help of a wealthy philanthropist and of a U.S. congressman. Perhaps that would not have been so odd if the philanthropist and the congressman lived in Warrenton and had occasion to get to know Samuel Johnson. But both lived in Prince William County to the northeast of Fauquier. Because Johnson later explained that a key part of the agreement was forged "at the instance of" the philanthropist, Matthew Harrison, one imagines that one day when Harrison was doing business in Fauquier County, he chanced upon a conversation with Edward Digges. Perhaps Johnson was there too, in the tavern, as Digges revealed that his slave Sam wished to purchase his freedom and that he, Digges, was inclined to allow him to do so since Sam was such a good fellow, such a steady worker, so honest, so upright, and so loyal. Harrison, extolled upon his death for his "benevolent deeds," his "pure . . . heart," and his "modesty," wanted to help and offered some advice. He suggested that Sam be transferred to a third party. That way the agreement reached would exist between two free people, legal persons, rather than between a slave and his owner. And Harrison had someone honorable in mind, Richard Brent, then serving in Congress as a Republican.[31]

Digges would transfer his slave to Brent upon the condition that when Sam—for that is how the whites with whom he dealt spoke of him—had paid his master an agreed-upon amount, Brent would then issue a deed of manumission. Although later the transaction would be described as one in which Sam had "contracted with . . . Edward Digges . . . for the purchase of his freedom," it is unlikely that Samuel Johnson signed anything. The agreement between Digges and Brent proved an awkward but workable solution to the legal conundrum of how a slave, who could not technically own anything or enter into a contract, could nevertheless purchase his freedom, an act that would require both engaging in a contract and acquiring property (himself). Other acts of manumission in Virginia similarly involved third parties, although such arrangements were not the norm. (Ordinarily, slaves and their masters simply ignored the prohibition on slaves' making contracts.) The involvement of so many people made the drawing up of the "contract" by which Samuel Johnson would earn his liberty a long, deliberate affair, not an act done lightly or impulsively.[32]

Surely Johnson felt some anxiety as he saved money to fulfill the terms of the agreement. He had to have wondered what would happen if Digges or Brent failed to do his part. And perhaps he was let down that after the contract had been made, his life continued more or less as it had. Samuel Johnson—as he always referred to himself, though sometimes it was transcribed as Johnston—remained in Warrenton, kept working at the tavern, and was still commonly known as "Digges' Sam."

What were Harrison's and Brent's motives? They did not oppose slavery, as did some Methodists and most Quakers. Neither of them seems to have registered any antislavery feelings, and both owned slaves. Brent, who owned sixty-five people in 1810, had once advertised for the return of an enslaved man, Eleck, who ran away in 1795.[33] Rather, living with slavery meant that they understood its complexities better than we often do today. For them, allowing a few slaves to earn their liberty made the system appear more just and allowed emancipators to appear benevolent. Freedom for some might even work to shore up slavery's foundations if other enslaved people saw their own emancipation as a possibility. The hope of freedom could encourage slaves to conduct themselves better, not worse, since slaves might try to earn their liberty through good behavior. At least, that is what some masters believed. They thought that slaves' working for freedom by being loyal and dutiful would divert their desire for liberty into safe channels rather than rebellious ones. This logic betrayed a troubling premise: allowing even a few slaves to purchase their freedom indicated that slaves had a natural desire for liberty and that enslaving them was therefore brutal and unjust.[34]

With his upright, loyal, honest behavior, and also because of his light skin, Samuel Johnson appeared to many whites to be just the sort of enslaved man whose emancipation, or rather self-purchase, might benefit the community at large.

He was about twenty-seven years old in 1802 and had to raise five hundred dollars to earn his liberty, for that was the amount he and Digges had settled on. Five hundred dollars was a substantial sum — a compliment, in a way, since it reflected Johnson's worth. By comparison, when Johnson purchased a half-acre plot of land with a house on it in 1818, it cost three hundred dollars, and in the 1810s, the commonwealth's attorney (like a district attorney) for Fauquier County earned an annual salary of $270.[35] Because he held a less lucrative position than the highly skilled artisan slaves, who could often earn significant amounts of money doing work on their own time, it would take Samuel Johnson many years to earn his liberty. Nevertheless, he began saving, penny by penny, nickel by nickel.[36] He continued saving even as whites' reactions to Gabriel's Rebellion, the conspiracies of 1802, and more general changes in early nineteenth-century Virginia threatened the 1782 manumission law and therefore Johnson's ability to free himself.

Protest against the law had come first from citizens of King and Queen County, who in the legislative session that followed the discovery of Gabriel's plot submitted a petition that blamed "our Disturbed & Distressed Situation" on the "Law for Freeing Negroes." The King and Queen County petitioners typified the many white Virginians who believed, somewhat unreasonably and despite the evidence, that free blacks would be the germ of any rebellion, which would pit not just slaves but all blacks against all whites. Fearing race war, some white Virginians decided that they ought to return to the policy of the colonial era, when they had kept the descendants of Africans under tight control through slavery and allowed only a very few to become free. Specifically, the King and Queen County petitioners asked that the 1782 law be repealed and that in the future slaves be freed only for "Meritorious Services," as the colonial statute had provided.[37]

Although they did not act on the King and Queen County petition, the legislators did three years later, in 1803, take up a bill that required all slaves subsequently freed to leave the state or forfeit their freedom.[38] They did not pass that bill into law but considered another restriction on manumission in 1805, a bill "to prevent the emancipation of slaves within this commonwealth."[39] As the state legislature contemplated this plan to abolish manumission altogether, Samuel Johnson's prospects for freedom looked increasingly dim.

Under such circumstances a man who had saved some cash and hoped for freedom might have considered running away. It would not have been too difficult for Johnson to steal a horse from a stable near the courthouse, to ride the county's dirt roads, to head north to Pennsylvania. And at least one member of his family did flee to Pennsylvania decades later.

But to Samuel Johnson, Fauquier was home. He had at some point married, probably around the time he contracted for his freedom. By about 1803 his wife, Patty, had given birth to a son they named Sam, who then became the property of Patty's owner (whose name has been lost).[40] Samuel Johnson would not go alone, abandoning his wife and child. And running away together would have meant taking the infant, a dangerous and difficult choice. If they were caught, Patty and the baby might be punished by being sold somewhere Johnson could not follow. Like many other African Americans, Johnson struggled and suffered to remain in his home with his family.

Samuel Johnson seems to have felt that leaving Virginia for freedom among people and places unknown would only replicate the journey that had brought Africans to America: separation from one's home, family, and local culture. He was not alone. Some Virginia slaves, faced as Johnson was with departing Virginia to be free, rejected leaving. Lucinda, for example, refused to leave King George County as had been directed by the will of her benevolent owner, who had emancipated all her slaves. As "dear" as freedom was to Lucinda, her husband was more dear. In 1813 Lucinda chose slavery over freedom, asking to become the slave of her husband's owner so that she could remain with him.[41] Lucinda's refusal to leave Virginia for freedom was unusual but not unique. Stephen Bias, a sixty-two-year-old freed slave who had emigrated to the free state of Ohio, also preferred Virginia. He found that "so marked was the difference in the manners and habits of the people of Ohio when contrasted with those amongst whom he had been raised that he could not remain amongst them with the least happiness or contentment." He declared that he would "prefer being sold into slavery in Virginia to being again compelled to emigrate to & reside in the state of Ohio."[42]

That choice—slavery in Virginia or freedom elsewhere—was the terrible dilemma presented to Afro-Virginians after 1806, when the legislature, having defeated the 1805 bill that banned manumission, passed instead a law that continued to allow manumission but only if the freed slaves departed Virginia within a year after they had been liberated. Those who stayed illegally could be taken by county officials and sold back into slavery.

At that point, four years after making the agreement with Digges and still scrimping and saving to accumulate the five hundred dollars he needed to be free, Samuel Johnson had a number of options. He could accept the terms of the new law, continue to work toward his freedom, and leave Virginia after he had earned his liberty. That would entail leaving behind Patty, Sam, and all the people and places he had known and running the risk that he might find himself miserable among those of different manners and habits. Of great importance, it would also mean leaving behind his connections with the white people who had helped him and who, he hoped, would continue to do so. In a new place he would have no aid or assistance from the likes of Richard Brent or Matthew Harrison. Alternatively, he could ignore the law, stay in Fauquier illegally after his emancipation, and risk being sold back into slavery. Many people did this, usually without consequence, but Johnson knew a lot of lawyers, did things by the book, and dared not take the risk. Johnson could also choose to accept defeat and remain in Virginia legally but enslaved. Or he could continue saving and hope for special dispensation from the legislature, that is, permission to remain in Virginia as an exception to the terms of the 1806 law.

Perhaps because his job in the tavern brought him into contact with so many of Fauquier County's leading men, especially its lawyers, judges, and representatives to the state legislature, Johnson knew that the latter was possible. His decision to try to gain an exemption from the 1806 statute also reflected his personality: dignified, honorable, and trusting that those to whom he was good and loyal would in turn be good to him.

In the fall of 1811, after nearly a decade of savings had yielded the requisite five hundred dollars, Samuel Johnson's white friends helped him draft a petition to the Virginia state legislature. By then his family had grown larger and included a daughter, Lucy.[43] The legislature's response to his petition would determine not only Samuel Johnson's future but the futures of Patty, Sam Jr., and Lucy too. Success would mean freedom, and failure would mean having to choose between several terrible options: slavery in Virginia; uncertain freedom and the possibility of re-enslavement as an illegal Virginia resident; or exile to some other state, separated from his wife and children.

"To the Honorable the Speaker and Members of the House of Delegates and Senate of Virginia," the petition began, "Sam: free mulatto respectfully represents that . . . as far back as ten years ago [he] contracted with his then master Edward Digges Sr. of Fauquier County for the purchase of his freedom." The petition went on to explain that Matthew Harrison had suggested that Digges convey Samuel Johnson to a third party, Richard Brent, on the condition that as soon as Sam paid the five hundred dollars he "should be free." Because Richard Brent had served several terms in Virginia's General Assembly, some of the delegates who had to decide on the petition knew Brent personally, and surely all would have heard of the man who had served three terms in the U.S. Congress and was in 1811 one of Virginia's two U.S. senators.[44]

Aside from the appearance of such important names as Brent's and Harrison's in the petition's first paragraph, "Sam's petition," as the clerk labeled it, employed another powerful rhetorical strategy, calling Johnson a "free mulatto," even though he was still enslaved. The term likely also indicated the quasi-free state in which he had been living. Digges may have been allowing Johnson to manage his own affairs, perhaps even to draw a salary and live

Samuel Johnson's 1811 petition to the Virginia legislature, front. SJP 1811.

on his own while he was saving the money he needed. It also seems that by 1811 Warrenton residents viewed Johnson as free; the petition's scribe wrote, but then crossed out, that he had been "free" since he had accumulated the requisite money twelve months earlier.

The petition further explained Samuel Johnson's situation. It had been "by great exertion himself and through the aid of benev-

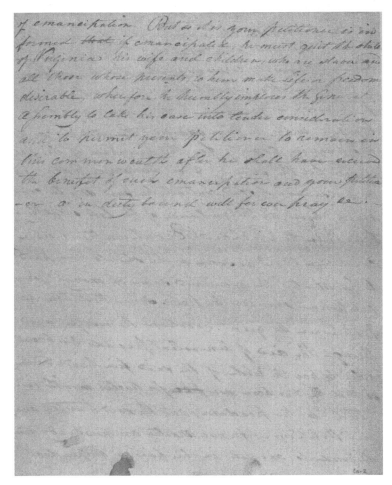

Samuel Johnson's 1811 petition to the Virginia legislature, back. Note the absence of a signature. SJP 1811.

olent friends" that he had accumulated the five hundred dollars. His former master was now ready to "execute" the contract. But if freed, Johnson would have to "quit the state of Virginia, his wife and children, who are slaves, and all those whose presents [*sic*] to him make life or freedom desirable." Johnson's petition begged for an alternative to exile, to separation from his beloveds. He wanted permission "to remain in this commonwealth after he shall have received the benefit of . . . emancipation."

Because Samuel Johnson, like most slaves, was illiterate and never signed any legal document with more than an X to signify his assent, the unsigned petition must have been penned by one of his "benevolent friends."[45] Even so, Johnson probably discussed the petition with the author and likely heard a draft read aloud. The resulting document painted a multifaceted portrait of its subject, combining Warrenton whites' view of Sam with Samuel Johnson's self-perception. On the one hand, the petition referred to him only as "Sam," although he already was known by his full name. In this way it revealed that Johnson's white helpers and friends saw him as they saw other slaves who, like children, went by diminutives: Sam rather than Samuel, Betsy rather than Elizabeth, Judy rather than Judith. On the other hand, the petition portrayed Samuel Johnson as a dignified human being. Designed to convince a group disposed not to grant such requests, it emphasized Johnson's "exertions" (he was a good worker), his family (perhaps the legislators would sympathize with not wanting to leave one's wife and children), and the willingness of white people to support and help him (which suggested that he was a good, trustworthy man who would be welcomed rather than reviled by his white neighbors). Rather than describing a slave, someone who was lowly, dependent, and childlike, the petition depicted an upright, hard-working, free family man, a person not unlike the legislators themselves, a person toward whom they might feel sympathy.

To further sway the legislature, Johnson and his white friends included a testimonial signed by thirty-eight members of the town's white community, including Thaddeus Norris, who noted that Johnson "has served [him] . . . for 12 or 15 years." Those thirty-eight men accounted for much of the town's adult white male population; in 1820 Warrenton contained about that number of white male heads of household and a total of 129 white males over the age of fifteen.[46] The large proportion of the town's white men who endorsed Samuel Johnson's request described him as a "color'd man"—not a slave but a man—who "has liv'd for many years at Fauquier Court House," where they also lived. They considered it "both a duty and a pleasure . . . to testify to the extraordinary merit of the applicant" because having "known him for a long time in the situation of principal servant in a considerable tavern," they found him "constantly and uniformly Diligent sober accommodating faithful and honest." These were precisely the qualities "essential to form a valuable citizen." Moreover, they wanted him to stay in Fauquier: "he wishes to remain amongst us, we wish it also." Finally, since Sam was a model slave, granting him the reward of freedom "would afford a wise encouragement to others to behave as he has behav'd, and by a like fidelity and honesty to deserve as he deserves."[47]

To further bolster the petition and testimonial, Samuel Johnson's previous owner, Edward Digges, wrote a note emphasizing that his agreement to free Johnson took place "before the passage of the Act of 1806 inhibiting the emancipation of Slaves" and would have "been carried into full effect had the money been paid before" 1806.[48] That was a good strategy, since in other cases the legislators seem to have given weight to claims to freedom that had in some way originated before 1806.[49]

Hundreds of slaves in the years between the 1806 law and the Civil War petitioned the legislature as Johnson did, but few marshaled such strong evidence in their favor, and most did not succeed.[50] Samuel Johnson's petition was remarkable, not because it claimed Sam was a loyal and honest slave—almost all petitions requesting permission to remain did that—but because it was backed by a large percentage of the local white men and, implicitly, by a U.S. senator.

As the delegates considered his request along with all the other legislation they dealt with that winter, Samuel Johnson awaited word regarding their decision. The petition had arrived in the House of Delegates in Richmond in mid-December, and Digges forwarded his note about a month later. In the week between Christmas and New Year's Day, a traditional time of rest for slaves, Johnson must have wondered whether the next holiday season would find him free. Finally, in early 1812, after the Committee on the Courts of Justice approved the petition, one of the legislators drew up a bill in accord with Samuel Johnson's request.[51]

Even after the House of Delegates passed the bill allowing Johnson to remain in Virginia, it could not become law until the state senate approved it also. Here again Samuel Johnson's special position and wide reputation proved crucial. One of the representatives from Fauquier County, Colonel Thornton Buckner, spoke to John Scott, then serving as Fauquier County's state senator, who in turn urged his senate colleague William Poindexter to see the bill to passage in the upper house. Scott, a local lawyer, had known Samuel Johnson for years and assured Senator Poindexter that "the indulgence asked for cannot be extended to a more deserving object." Johnson, he said, was "a man of the first respectability in the county." Scott described the petitioner's attributes at some length: "Sam is a fellow of most unblemished character. In point of honesty he is second to no man white or black. He has succeeded in attaching to him all who know him." Finally, in his capacity as "a waiter in the Tavern at Fauq'r Ct House his removal would be a public loss."[52] When in the spring of 1812 the state senate passed the bill allowing Johnson to remain in Virginia, one of Fauquier County's representatives probably forwarded the news to Edward Digges, who told Johnson. Thus a number of powerful white men came together to help Samuel Johnson gain the right to be free in his home state.

The special law passed just for him said that he could remain in Virginia if liberated, but it did not actually emancipate him; he still needed Richard Brent to draft the deed of manumission. That did not take place until August 2, 1812, because Richard Brent was in Washington, D.C., until July, when the congressional session ended amid great concern over relations with Great Britain. Apparently, Johnson's employer, Thaddeus Norris, along with a man named Thomas Moore, traveled to Prince William County to see Brent and to witness the deed, which they brought back to Warrenton. Perhaps Samuel Johnson accompanied them, but if he had we might expect the deed to have revealed more of Johnson's story than it did. The deed said nothing of the deal Johnson had made with Edward Digges, nothing of the legislature's act. If one were to judge only from the deed, one would think that Samuel Johnson had nothing to do with his own freedom except that he had performed with "fidelity diligence and good behavior." And yet Johnson was not completely invisible: unlike any of the other documents of that year, the deed of manumission mentioned his full name, referring to him as "my Slave Sam called and known by the name of Samuel Johnson of Norris's Tavern."[53]

Still, it was not enough. The document could be challenged as a forgery if it were not proved in court. Either the signer of the document, Richard Brent, or the witnesses, Norris and Moore, had to swear before the justices that the deed was legitimate. Since Brent chose not to travel to Fauquier's courthouse, the burden fell on Norris and Moore who, on August 25, 1812, stood before the judges and swore on the Bible that the deed of manumission Samuel Johnson presented to the court was a legitimate document, since they had witnessed Brent sign it.

None of the legal records mention Johnson's presence, but it is almost impossible to imagine that he was not there. He watched and listened as the justices ordered this deed, like so many others, to be recorded in the county deed book by the clerk. Later, after the clerk had copied it for the county records, he would return the original document to Samuel Johnson. Johnson would need to keep that copy, his "free papers," to prove his status in the future.

The court transaction on August 25, 1812, probably took only a couple of minutes. There was no ceremony, no elaborate ritual—just a legal document ordered by the judges to be recorded by the clerk.⁵⁴ It was a deceptively ordinary transaction, not so different from the many other transactions that made up the business of the day. A casual observer, lost for a moment in his own thoughts, might have missed it. And yet it was that certification of the deed of manumission that finally made Samuel Johnson the free man he had so long yearned to be. With that mundane transaction, he could be assured of his liberty. Only then could he walk outside into the summer day with the lightness a free man feels, with the air moving easily into his free man's lungs, the warm August breeze kissing his free skin.

When Samuel Johnson walked out of the courthouse on that day of his rebirth from slavery to freedom, he acquired a self. Of course, in his own eyes, he had always been a person, an individual. In his own eyes, he was Samuel Johnson, "mulatto." As a slave, however, he had been known merely as "Sam" and had been someone else's property. Free now, he became publicly and legally what he had already known himself to be: a man, a man with a full name, a man no longer owned by others, self-possessed.

Rather than the end of his story, however, the moment of Johnson's rebirth into freedom marked the beginning of a greater quest, the first step on a path he had envisioned for himself and his family. Until Patty and their children, Sam Jr. and Lucy, were all free, Samuel Johnson could not consider his job done. One of the greatest fears of anyone with an enslaved spouse was that he or she might at any time be sold away. Without the basic assurance of white married couples that they could, if they wished, remain together, Samuel and Patty lived with great anxiety. Even worse, they could not provide for their children as free families could. They could not ensure that their children would learn useful skills and gain a modicum of education. Because the children were themselves the property of another, Samuel and Patty also could not exert the kind of parental authority whites took for granted. If Sam Jr. or Lucy did something wrong, it would be their owner, Patty's owner, who would punish them. In essence, to have one's family owned by another was to be emasculated, stripped of the responsibilities, duties, and powers of a man: to provide for his family, discipline his children, and be their representative in the world. Samuel Johnson could not be the man of the house when that house was empty of all but himself.

Thus, from the very moment he became free, Samuel Johnson set about acquiring the same status for his family. It would prove to be an even more tortuous, and torturous, journey than the one that had brought him, finally, to freedom outside Fauquier's courthouse.

CHAPTER TWO

among an anomalous population

THE FIRST STEP SAMUEL JOHNSON had to take to free his family was to purchase them. They would not then be free. They still would be slaves. But with Johnson as their owner they would not be sold away from him. Even if legally enslaved, Johnson's family could, if he owned them, act as free people and join Warrenton's small free black community. They could, in other words, enter that complicated space that in early nineteenth-century Virginia lay between slavery and freedom and helped define what race meant.

Samuel Johnson acted rapidly to buy his family. It had taken a decade to acquire the five hundred dollars necessary to gain his own freedom, but it took only three years to earn enough to buy Patty, Sam Jr., and Lucy. His only explanation for how he had managed to raise the money so quickly was that he had pursued the same "line of conduct" and practiced the same "industry, Eoconomy [*sic*], and general good deportment" that had served him well earlier.[1] Oddly, although the purchase of his family was so crucial, it appears that no record of the transaction remains. Most likely he bought all three from the same person, Patty's owner, probably paying at least several hundred dollars for them.

Once Samuel had purchased Patty and the children, the Johnsons took the form of a number of other early nineteenth-century Afro-Virginian families—a free man and the wife and children he owned as slaves. Frank Gowen in Amelia County

32

and Bowling Clark in Campbell County, for example, similarly owned their families.[2] Most of the free black slaveowners of the nineteenth century—and there were not very many to begin with—owned family members and not unrelated slaves for profit.[3] Holding one's family as slaves seemed to be the best choice in an era in which emancipation ordinarily equaled exile. But such families were heartbreakingly vulnerable. When Gowen died in 1809, his family were his property and not his heirs. As slaves who now belonged to no one, they were slated to be sold, with the proceeds going into the public coffers. Johnson, with his awareness of the laws and with all his lawyer friends, surely knew that such a horrible fate could befall Patty and the children if he died suddenly. Even giving them to someone else in his will did not necessarily protect them; Johnson could not be certain how that future owner might behave.

So Johnson returned to the course that had brought his own right to remain in Virginia: petitioning the legislature. His petition of December 1815 mentioned his recent emancipation, his purchase of his wife and children, and his desire that they all should be free in Virginia "instead of their having to flee" if he emancipated them. This freedom, he said, was the "end to which all [his] anxious labour and privations" had "been directed."[4] But the lawmakers allowed his petition "to lie" on the table, meaning that after it was read in committee, the members took no action on it. It was neither rejected nor approved. It simply died.

Perhaps the state lawmakers failed to act on Johnson's petition because they were trying to enforce a new law that turned over to the county courts the responsibility for deciding whether free blacks could remain in Virginia, a move apparently designed to save themselves the trouble of passing special laws for people like Samuel Johnson. The new law even allowed the county courts to extend permission to remain in Virginia to the "emancipated wife or husband" of the original petitioner or "to his or her emancipated children" if the original petitioner had been freed for some act of "extraordinary merit." But the law also said that the county court's decision was final and that there could be no appeal.[5]

If Johnson wanted to take advantage of the new law, he would first have to free his family, and then they would have to appear in court and ask the county justices for permission to remain. Few Fauquier County free blacks ever applied to the county court for permission to remain, but the court showed itself relatively favorable toward such requests. Barnett Toliver, for example, applied in 1816 for permission to stay and received it the following year, and newly freed people Jack and Hannah along with their two children also received permission to remain in 1817.[6] Samuel Johnson could reasonably expect that his family would be similarly favored, especially since Johnson had already been given legislative permission to stay.

But then again, applying to the county court for permission to remain provided no guarantee, and Johnson must have worried about the absence of any appeal process should the original petition be denied, as his 1815 petition to the legislature had been. In addition, if he knew what happened to Barnett Toliver, then he also knew that Betsy Davis, who had been emancipated along with Toliver, saw her case drag on for more than a year with no resolution. She never did receive permission to remain, although she still lived in the county two decades later.[7] Johnson thus decided to play it safe and make sure *before* he emancipated them that his family could stay in Virginia as free people. Legal changes of 1819 would only have confirmed his decision not to work through the county court, for in that year amendments to the law imposed greater restrictions on county courts' actions, including the requirement that the commonwealth's attorney support any petition to remain and that the petitioner gain the unanimous support of the county magistrates.[8] Johnson thus chose to direct his petition to the legislature and not the county court, but he did not take up that project until 1820.

In the meantime, the Johnson family in the late 1810s lived as if they were free, even though they were not. The laws regarding freedom and slavery had real force, and Patty and the children's legal status as slaves had real effect. The laws regarding free black people, or "free negroes" in contemporary parlance, also shaped their lives, even though only Samuel was legally free. In their day-to-day experience it was not laws, however, that primarily determined what their race or status meant. How people behaved toward them and how they behaved toward others more greatly affected their lives. In Warrenton, Virginia, as elsewhere in the Atlantic world, race was a way of seeing, and depended not only on one's vantage point but also on the particular scene one surveyed.

Samuel Johnson's view was oriented toward his family; he focused his attention on all the practical tasks of being a father and husband. After he had purchased his family and their enslavement became a technicality rather than an overwhelming burden, he worked to build a life and home with Patty and the children. More than a decade after they married, Patty and Samuel could now finally share a household. They could do the things white couples took for granted. Each could learn the other's daily routines and rhythms, and could come to recognize more clearly the signals that indicated a particular mood. Together, they could celebrate the little triumphs and mourn the small defeats of their domestic life. Particularly important, they could now take full responsibility for rearing their children, a responsibility that legally and practically had fallen to Patty's owner before Samuel had purchased them.

The most important choice they made regarding their children was that Lucy, who was ten years old in 1815, should be brought up in the house of the tavern keepers Thaddeus and Ann Norris, instead of in her parents' home. Their choice was not so unusual; a number of other African American or poor white families of the era sent their daughters to work in other people's houses as "apprentices" to learn housewifery, continuing an Anglo-American tradition in which children above the age of six or seven were understood to be workers.[9] But it seems that the agreement between the Johnsons and Norrises was more than a business calculation, more than a way to relieve the Johnsons of the costs of raising Lucy, and more than a way to give the Norrises an extra hand around the house. Many years later, well after Lucy was grown, Ann Norris described how she had raised Lucy "in my house" and how she had taught Lucy "all the principles of honour, honesty, industry and virtue" so that the grown-up Lucy "stands as fair as any other female in the county."[10]

Those words help explain why, after working so hard to purchase his family, Samuel Johnson did not keep them together under one roof. The Norrises—white, literate people of the middling classes—could provide Lucy important advantages that the Johnsons could not. Ann Norris could teach Lucy a more refined version of housewifery than Patty Johnson likely learned as an enslaved woman. Under Ann Norris's tutelage, Lucy might have learned the genteel task of needlework in addition to the more basic skills of spinning and sewing. Ann, but not Patty, could teach Lucy to read and to write at least a bit. As an adult, Lucy, unlike her parents, could sign her own name.[11] Furthermore, being raised by white people along with their own children might have given Lucy more standing in the community.

Unfortunately, the arrangement led to significant conflict between Johnson and his employer, for the Norrises seemed to want more power over Lucy than Samuel Johnson was willing to allow. Or maybe Thaddeus Norris, who by 1820 had been declared a lunatic, was already acting strangely, and Johnson wanted his daughter out of Norris's house.[12] In 1818 the conflict, whatever it was, came to a head, and Johnson sued Norris in detinue, meaning that he asked for the return of his property (Lucy) from Norris. Two oddities in this suit stand out. One is that nowhere do the

House of Thaddeus Norris, built 1816. Lucy Johnson grew up in this large house, now a commercial building on Waterloo Street (formerly Jail Street) in Warrenton. The ornate porch likely dates from a later era. Photo by Eva Sheppard Wolf.

remaining court records refer to Johnson as a man of color or to Lucy as his daughter. The case appears as an ordinary transaction between two men fighting over possession of a slave. The second is that the suit did not result in a permanent cleavage between the Johnsons and the Norrises. Lucy apparently continued to live in the Norris home even after Norris admitted his guilt, Johnson won the suit, and the court awarded Johnson money for damages and costs.[13]

The lawsuit also raises the possibility that Thaddeus Norris had been the owner of Patty, Sam Jr., and Lucy, and that he had held on to Lucy until Samuel Johnson had paid all the money he owed for her—or perhaps there was some dispute over when that money had been paid. The suit indicated that Lucy, as a slave, was worth a lot: four hundred dollars.[14] If Johnson had fudged

things a bit in his 1815 petition when he had declared that he had
purchased his family—if Lucy was then still unpaid for—that
would help explain why Johnson in 1815–19 did not apply to the
county court for permission for his family to remain in Virginia.

Whatever the details of the arrangements between Samuel
Johnson and Thaddeus Norris, and whatever the precise causes of
the mysterious 1818–19 lawsuit—the full records of which no longer exist—things turned out all right.[15] Lucy was never far away
from her family, and she did learn things from Ann Norris that
her parents could not have taught her. Ann's later words, that she
brought Lucy up "as one of my own children," also suggest that
she developed real affection for Lucy. To speak of a girl of color
as being like one of the white Norris children was to cross one
of Virginia's racial lines, an act of transgression that Ann Norris
seems to have made easily, and one she shared with more people
than we might expect.

One thing is clear about the Johnson family's circumstances
in 1818: it was not because Samuel Johnson was impoverished
that Lucy lived with the Norrises, as was the case for many other
families who bound out their daughters as apprentice house-
wives. Instead, Johnson continued his financial move upward.
By the end of 1818 he had saved enough money, three hundred
dollars, to purchase a half acre of land with a house on it just
outside Warrenton's town limits.[16] The house and land lay near
the well square, a convenient location, since the family would
not have to go far for water.[17] And while technically outside
Warrenton, the lot lay only a few blocks' walk from Norris's
tavern.

The purchase brought with it new neighbors. The Johnsons
lived not in a ghetto of free black people, but next door to a white
couple of standing, John A. W. and Maria L. Smith, educated
people to whom they could turn for advice. John A. W. Smith
was the clerk of the Fauquier County court from 1821 to 1832, and
as the person who recorded the court's business, he was familiar

with legal forms, traditions, and procedures. He would be able to supply invaluable advice to the Johnson family. He was also the purveyor of fire insurance for the town, and perhaps Samuel Johnson bought some.[18]

By 1820, when the children were in their mid-teens and Johnson in his mid-forties, Johnson headed a household of six people, which made his the largest free black household in the vicinity. Living with him were Patty, an enslaved man over the age of forty-five, and three people of color: a boy under the age of fourteen, a young man between fourteen and twenty-six, and a man between twenty-six and forty-five. These bare facts found in the 1820 U.S. Census are frustratingly silent on all sorts of relevant matters. We do not know the name or anything else about the older enslaved man who lived under Johnson's roof. Perhaps he was there as a hired servant, or perhaps Johnson had purchased him as he had purchased Patty and the children, so that he could live as a free person. The younger people in the household are equally perplexing. The boy between fourteen and twenty-six years old may have been Sam Jr., but perhaps he, like Lucy, lived elsewhere. The best guess is that several of the residents in the house were tenants whose rent brought the Johnsons a bit of cash and whose presence made Samuel Johnson a landlord.[19] Not rich, then, but the Johnsons were not destitute. And they were free — almost.

Race as a legal reality powerfully limited the freedoms the Johnsons had acquired after Samuel purchased his liberty, his family, a house, and land. Even though Samuel, Patty, and the children appeared and probably felt themselves to be living as free people, key discrepancies between their lives and those of white Virginians shadowed them. One was the fact that by law he and Patty were not actually married. Slaves did hold their own marriage ceremonies, often involving jumping over a broomstick together, but Virginia's laws did not recognize such unions — one of the ways in which slavery dehumanized. Even after Samuel

Johnson had become free and purchased Patty, their union remained extralegal because she was still a slave. Its extralegal nature means that no record exists of Samuel and Patty's marriage,
although it seems likely that they wed just around the turn of
the century when Johnson arranged for his freedom. It may have
been that the occasion of his marriage and his desire to head a
household first sparked Johnson's quest for liberty. Judging from
his later actions, his marriage, despite its lack of legal standing,
held deep meaning for him. Johnson worked hard to be the kind
of husband and father that Virginia's dominant culture valued.
That Virginia's legislators thwarted his efforts in 1815 when they
denied permission to free Patty and the children served as a bit-
ter reminder that under the law, color often mattered more than
behavior.

Under the law, color mattered quite a lot. Virginia law circumscribed the Johnson family's lives as they had circumscribed
Afro-Virginians' lives since the seventeenth century. As early
as 1643, a generation after the colony's founding, the laws of
Virginia had discriminated between free people based on their
color. It was in the mundane but important domain of tax law
that the distinction first showed up. In specifying who counted
as workers, or "tithes," upon whom taxes had to be paid, the
1643 tax law included free black women, but not white women.
Free black families thus had to pay higher taxes than free white
families until free black people successfully protested this provision in 1769.[20] The differential tax provision of 1643 indicated
some of the negative feelings whites held toward blacks even
at a time when Virginia contained only a few Africans. The
legislators of the time saw black women as significantly *different* from white women — as laborers and therefore as a kind of
commodity.[21]

Lawmakers in the late seventeenth century enacted additional racial distinctions that continued into the period in
which the Johnsons lived. These laws, which created both race

and slavery as legal categories, helped to support racial slavery both when it began to dominate the economy in the late seventeenth century and 150 years later during Samuel Johnson's lifetime. Legislators created race partly by lumping all "Negros, Mulattos, and Indians, bond or free," together into one group, rather than distinguishing civil abilities according to slave or free status.[22]

Who counted as "Negro" or "Indian" seemed to be obvious, but the group to which Johnson belonged, "Mulattos," needed definition. Lawmakers first provided a definition in 1705, stating that anyone with one Indian grandparent or one "Negro" great-grandparent would legally be a "mulatto" and not a white person, and therefore disqualified from "any place of public trust or power." In the Revolutionary period they modified the definition so that anyone with one "Negro" grandparent would count as a "mulatto," but a person with only one "Negro" great-grandparent, such as Thomas Jefferson's children with Sally Hemings, would be legally white. By the time Samuel Johnson purchased his family, these legal racial categories—"Negro," "mulatto," "Indian"—and their implicit opposite, "white," had a long, and mostly unquestioned, history.[23]

Thus it was old news that being "Negro" or "mulatto" in Johnson's time prevented a man from protecting himself and his family as white men could. He could not legally own a gun without obtaining from the court a special license, which white people did not need.[24] If he did obtain a license for a gun, he might still find himself or his family threatened in one way or another by local white residents. And if something were to happen, if a white person assaulted him or Patty, or took any property he owned, he could not testify against that person in court. Since 1744, the law had stated that black Virginians, free as well as enslaved, could only testify against other "Negro" or "mulatto" people.[25] That law gave whites broad latitude to act with impunity toward Afro-Virginians. The Revolutionary period's lawmakers, who liberalized some of Virginia's slave and race code, nevertheless preserved the restriction on giving testimony.[26] In doing so, they signaled that white society still did not see mistreating black people as a *crime*—dishonorable, perhaps, in some cases but not a crime of which one could be accused in court. As a result, enslaved Virginians might find themselves to be better protected than free blacks because slaves' owners could testify in court against other white people.

Being a free black person left one quite vulnerable, subject to many of the same legal restrictions as slaves but without an owner who would have an interest in safeguarding his or her property. Like slaves, free blacks could be punished corporally for crimes that when committed by a white person had lesser consequences. A free black person, like a slave, could receive thirty lashes with a whip if he or she were to "lift his or her hand" to a white person, except in cases of self-defense when "wantonly assaulted." Black Virginians, unlike white Virginians, could have "one ear nailed to the pillory" and after an hour have "the said ear . . . cut off" if they gave "false testimony." Samuel Johnson and other emancipated slaves, but not white people, also had to worry about a provision of the 1782 manumission law that stated that freed slaves could be hired out by county officials if they failed to pay their taxes. Free blacks also had fewer opportunities than did free whites. For example, free black orphans did not have to be taught reading and writing as white orphans did. Lawmakers did not want to promote black literacy lest it give black people too much power.[27]

But, as Johnson's actions attest, free black Virginians did have all the same property rights as whites and many other basic civil abilities. They could buy and sell land or slaves (usually their own families). They could enter into contracts and be parties to deeds. They could sue when one of their arrangements—like Johnson's agreement with Thaddeus Norris concerning Lucy—went awry. They could write wills. Virginia's courts recognized and upheld these rights even in an era that saw increasing restrictions on and increasing antipathy toward free blacks. In an 1838 case, the court said that a free black person "is at once entitled to acquire and enjoy property. His person is under the protection of the laws, and he has a right to sue for injuries done to person or to property."[28] It is a testament to how much Anglo-American law valued and focused on property rights that, unlike personal rights, property rights extended to free people of color. In fact, the only significant legal protection specifically accorded to free blacks was that they could not be stolen and sold into slavery: they could not be turned (back) into property.[29]

Johnson took good advantage of the abilities he had under the law. He bought additional land, adding for $175 in 1822 another half acre that adjoined his original purchase.[30] In later years he was party to additional deeds and sued in court to obtain property he thought was due to him. And he wrote a will before he died. None of these things would have been possible as a slave.

Yet in the details of some of these transactions, the business dealings of a free person, we see again how race entered the picture. The 1818 deed by which he first purchased land described Johnson as "a free man of colour of the County of Fauquier." Those words were meant, presumably, to help identify and distinguish him from other Samuel Johnsons, but "Samuel Johnson of Warrenton" would have done the same thing. White Virginians, in this case the person who drafted the deed, simply saw people in terms of race.

Similarly, in fulfilling one of the great social obligations of free people, paying taxes, Johnson was again marked by color. First, he had to pay in 1815 a special tax on free black men. Then, because of his color, he did not pay taxes through most of the 1820s. At that time, the state collected taxes on personal property, including slaves, and real estate.[31] Johnson had both personal property and real estate, but the county tax collectors seem to have failed to notice him until 1829. In that year, Andrew Turner, the tax commissioner in charge of collecting personal property taxes, began to keep track of "free negroes" by listing them and their tax obligations separately in his book. Only when grouped with others into this special category did Johnson enter the tax collector's consciousness. Samuel Johnson began to pay land taxes the next year when a new tax commissioner, Thomas Ashby, noticed Johnson as the previous one had not and began to assess his land. That no record exists showing that Johnson paid taxes for most of the 1820s suggests that the tax commissioners of those years saw free blacks more as property than as property owners. Indeed most free blacks in town were quite poor.[32]

Samuel Johnson, despite being the wealthiest among Warrenton's free blacks, benefited in an odd way from whites' general disregard of free people of color. It was as if the white men who ran the county and did its business simply did not *see* most free Afro-Virginians when they surveyed the people around them. Color could be invisibility, as Ralph Ellison said of his own invisibility more than a century later.[33]

For the Johnson family, joining the free black community of Fauquier meant joining a group of people neither enslaved nor fully free who were discriminated against by law and often disparaged by the dominant group in society, free whites. Thomas Jefferson viewed free people of color to be "as incapable as children of taking care of themselves" and as "pests in society."[34] The white men of King and Queen County worried that the existence of free blacks would encourage racial "commixture," which they found "abhorrent."[35] And many white Virginians were convinced that free blacks threatened to upset the entire social order because they "will, no doubt, unite with the slaves" to foment insurrection.[36] In short, the white majority saw free blacks as "[i]nferior to the whites in intelligence & information; degraded by the stain which attaches to their colour; excluded from many civil privileges which the humblest white man enjoys, and denied all participation in the government."[37]

Although some Virginia cities, such as Richmond and Norfolk, were by 1810 home to true free black communities—hundreds of people living in close proximity who formed social, religious, and other ties with one another—in early nineteenth-century Fauquier County free blacks constituted "an anomalous population."[38] In 1810 the county included only about 350 free black individuals, less than 2 percent of the county's total population, in its 650 square miles.[39] In Warrenton, where Johnson lived, there were only twenty-three free black people in 1810 and twenty-two in 1820. But there were about three hundred slaves, out of a total town population of around six hundred in those years. Compared to Warrenton's other free black residents, Johnson was fortunate, for almost all of the other free black Warrentonians seem to have been separated from their enslaved families, or at least part of their families. Two-parent households were rare among the eleven free black households in town. Ruth Hughs and Fanny Levers, for example, each headed households that included several children, and Nace Piles, who was then over forty-five years old, lived alone, as did Sally Grayson.[40]

Perhaps because the free blacks of Fauquier County, and of Warrenton in particular, were so small in number, county officials long ignored their statutory obligation to keep an official register of them. Free black workers had been required to register with authorities starting in 1793, and a general registration law was on the books from 1801. Fauquier officials, instead of keeping the mandated register of free blacks, certified their freedom in county court. Afterward, the clerk presumably issued a certificate or marked their documents accordingly. When in 1817 officials began following the letter of the law and keeping a separate Register of Free Negroes with numbered entries, some people still showed up in court to have their freedom certified, but others tried to follow the new rules.[41]

Samuel Johnson, ever dutiful, was the third free black person to answer the call to register with the county clerk. His behavior showed a special attention to this intrusive regulation, since most of Warrenton's free blacks never registered at all. On Saturday, June 21, 1817, he appeared before the clerk who noted his age, about forty-two or forty-three years; his height, 5 feet 7 ¾ inches; his "colour," "Bright Mulatto"; and a few other features, including that he had a "Bushy head" with "no scars or marks perceivable."[42]

We can imagine the scene that produced this entry. Johnson came to the clerk, who sat in his office at the courthouse, and told him he was there to register. The clerk asked him his name and age. Johnson knew his age approximately, but not exactly. That was more than Nace Piles, Ralph Wormly, or John Burk knew. Their recorded ages of "[a]bout 60 years," "[a]bout 30 years," and "[a]bout 25 years" suggest that they had only a vague sense of how old they were and that perhaps the clerk rounded to the nearest half decade.[43] Not being sure of one's age, one's own vital statistics, marked a person as born in slavery, and demonstrated how an enslaved past continued to mark a free present. The level of accuracy in Johnson's recorded height, by contrast, suggests that the clerk measured him. Johnson likely stood still, straight, and compliant as the clerk did so. The clerk could assess Johnson's "bright" color without any particular measuring tool, but determining that Johnson had "no scars or marks perceivable" required him to get relatively close, to peer at Johnson's face, to walk around his body, and to ask to see his hands, his arms, his feet.

Johnson's unscarred body distinguished him from almost all the other free blacks who registered with the Fauquier County clerk and points to how, compared to other slaves, he had lived a relatively privileged life. Nace Piles, for instance, had a "scar just above the large joint of the forefinger of the left hand." Ralph Wormly had a scar "on the inside of the right arm, about the joint." Nancy White had "[t]wo scars on the left arm," and Celia had a "scar in the brow of the left eye" and one "on the wrist bone of the left hand."[44] These scars indicated lives that were hard on the body. The physical labor enslaved people did, including household labor, increased the odds of accidental injury. Corporal punishment by owners or overseers left scars too, and scars on the face—particularly the frequently mentioned scars on or above the eyebrows—may have come from being boxed in the head. Working as a waiter in a tavern had spared Johnson many of the physical if not the psychic brutalities of slavery.

Once he had registered, Johnson would have received a copy of his registration record, which he likely kept with his other vital paperwork, including the copy of his deed of manumission. Free Afro-Virginians guarded these papers closely and considered them to be of utmost importance. Charles Hughes, for example, complained to the white authorities when Richard Stone kept Hughes's registration paper. Recognizing the gravity of the matter, the court acted swiftly to compel Stone to return Hughes's free papers, and Hughes had them back within a month after the court first met. Again, race shaped how white people saw things. They understood free papers to be important and honored the law, but they also saw men of color as not really *men*: the summons for Richard Stone referred to Charles Hughes as "a free boy of colour" when Hughes was thirty-six years old.[45]

Samuel Johnson's papers guaranteed him certain rights as a free person while the fact that he needed them marked him, like Charles Hughes, as an outsider. On the one hand, free papers ensured that he could not be taken to jail simply for walking around alone in a place where he was not well known. Free papers kept Willis Grimes out of jail in Alexandria, for example, when his wife, Rachel, was locked up as a runaway slave; and the lack of free papers meant that Burril Bartlett, who said he was free, was nevertheless kept in jail until a white man paid the cost of his imprisonment—and the white man got to keep Burril Bartlett as a servant for one month.[46] White people, of course, needed no papers to prove their status and traveled the world with a sense of belonging that black Virginians by law did not have. Having to register with county officials thus formalized Samuel Johnson's and other free black Virginians' marginal status.

Though living on society's margins, Johnson and other free blacks in antebellum Virginia, especially in Fauquier County, had to form ties across the line separating free from slave and the line separating white from nonwhite. Sometimes, practicality forced such a situation, such as when roads needed to be built or repaired. The law required free men to work eleven days per year on the roads, or to pay a fee to hire a substitute. There they were, black and white men working and sweating together on the outskirts of Warrenton. The white men did not like it. They complained that they were "like a herd of negroes ordered from labour to labour," and asked to be exempted from road work.[47]

White Fauquier County men also did not like the unlicensed tavern run in 1826 by Nace Piles, who was then an old man of around seventy. In an era long before retirement benefits, Piles was still at work. It was an enslaved man, Anthony Grant, who gave evidence to the county's grand jury that Piles had sold "spirits by retail at his house . . . to be drank when sold without license." (It is worth pointing out that Grant, though enslaved, had a last name just as Johnson had. Surnames were more common among slaves than we normally assume; presumably, enslaved people chose names they liked or to which they had some sense of attachment.) Grant's testimony is spare, so we know little about what went on at Piles's tavern. But we can glean that the gatherings successfully took place away from the watchful eyes of whites, or else a white person would have been able to testify against Piles. Maybe the "very simple unmeaning countenance" that the court clerk saw when Piles registered in 1817 as a "free negro" bespoke a keen ability to keep secrets and to skirt the rules. We can further deduce that Piles catered to both enslaved and free blacks who shared a common social world. Together, after their very long days, they met at Piles's house to drink and talk, and perhaps to dance. This was not a private party, as Piles was not a host but a businessman, not a "simple" man at all.[48]

Piles appeared to be in quite a bit of trouble, his entrepreneurial spirit unappreciated by the authorities. But when the key witness, Grant, could not be found to give evidence at trial, the case had to be dismissed. Why, one wonders, would Grant's owner, Hancock Lee, tell the sheriff that Grant did not live in the commonwealth? Had Lee sold him to a slave trader, as so many owners did in that era, as punishment? Was that of more importance to Lee than seeing Piles's illegal tavern closed? Or, rather improbably, might Lee have had some interest in protecting Piles and so moved Grant out of state? Although we can never know the answer to these questions, we can see that white Virginians had difficulty enforcing the rigid separations they wanted to see in society: in this case, between slave and free.

Other people also challenged the part they were supposed to play in Virginia's social order. Sometimes, free black men formed families with white women, which violated a strong social taboo. (White men, by contrast, found that their sexual unions with black women were quietly accepted as part of the order of things.)[49] In 1816, a Fauquier County grand jury made a presentment against a free black man named Philip Hughes and a white woman named Lucy Edwards who, in the words of the court, lived together "in a state of fornication."[50] They had, in fact, been forced into this state of having sexual relations outside of marriage, since marriage between white and black people had been illegal since the colonial period. No additional legal papers shed light on what happened next—whether the Hughes-Edwards family had to move or whether they somehow avoided further prosecution—but the existence of another Philip Hughes, born about a year after the grand jury made its presentment, suggests that at least Lucy Edwards remained in Fauquier County and raised her son. The younger Philip Hughes, as the registrar of free blacks noted, had light skin (he was a "bright mulatto") and, likely taking after his white mother, straight hair.[51] According to one history of white-black relations in Virginia, such consensual mixed-race unions were more common than we had thought.[52]

The enslaved Phill provides a further example of how difficult it was to enforce the lines that most white Virginians felt ought to divide society. Phill acted as a free man even though he was enslaved, much as Samuel Johnson may have acted in the years after he (or, technically, Richard Brent) contracted for his freedom. In the same court session in which the grand jury brought the case against Philip Hughes and Lucy Edwards, it also brought one against "Mary Taylor for suffering her Negro Slave Phill to hire himself and trade as a free man." Hiring out slaves on a temporary basis had become an important part of the slave economy in Virginia by the 1810s, but from 1792, it had been illegal for enslaved people to make hiring contracts themselves. White lawmakers did not want slaves to have control over their own labor, and they felt so strongly about it that they dictated that any owner who allowed a slave to hire out his or her own time would forfeit the slave, who would be sold by county officials, with the owner keeping about 70 percent of the sale price. And yet slave owners consistently violated that law and did allow their slaves to hire themselves out, as attested by the multiple criminal proceedings that remain in the record.[53]

Black and white men working together to fulfill their civic duties to maintain the roads; free and enslaved Afro-Virginians socializing together; white women living with and having children with black men; enslaved people behaving as free ones; enslaved people *becoming* free, as Samuel Johnson did—all these activities challenged the rigid two-race social order that so many white Virginians wished for, an order in which white, free people could rule confidently over black, enslaved ones.

And yet white Virginians participated in these and other violations of their ideal world. They made the rules that put white and black people together working on the roads. They usually looked the other way at illicit black taverns, and failed to successfully prosecute Nace Piles when they did turn their attention to him. They brought black children into white households and raised them alongside their own children, as Ann Norris did. White women sometimes chose black partners, and white men frequently did so. White people allowed their slaves to hire out their own time. And white people agreed to allow some black people, including Samuel Johnson, their freedom. Occasionally, all these transgressions began to really irritate someone, like Isaac Fosters, who headed the grand jury that brought presentments against Hughes and Edwards for fornication and against Mary Taylor for letting Phill hire himself out. (The fact that Fosters's grand jury made presentments, not indictments, indicates that the grand jury acted on its own, not in response to a prosecutor's charge.) But most of the time, white Virginians — and black ones too — accepted and lived with the complexities of their world.

They understood that race, as it operated in early nineteenth-century Virginia, did not simply create out of free blacks like Samuel Johnson a class of "slaves without masters" who stood between true slaves and free people.[54] Race and racism did not simply force free blacks back down toward the ranks of slaves. Rather, race, as individual people constituted it in their daily interactions, allowed many kinds of relationships between a community's members. Whites did dominate society and politics, and they made the discriminatory laws that sought to control black people. But as the story of the Johnson family and others in Virginia elucidates, the ways in which people lived their lives meant that race and its meanings varied, sometimes from moment to moment. When Philip Hughes and Lucy Edwards fell in love and began to live together, race meant one thing, and when Isaac Fosters got it in his head to stop them, it meant another. Race had legal meaning but was not so much a social or legal structure as something individuals themselves made, over and over again, as they worked, talked, loved, struggled — and brought grand jury presentments.

Knowing that in his own life and in the lives of many of his friends, neighbors, and acquaintances, race did not always need to form a barrier between people, Samuel Johnson pushed his way as best he could into a biracial world. His greatest undertaking was to gain for his family the right to remain in Virginia as free people. After the failed petition of 1815 and the following years of building a family life in Warrenton, Johnson refocused his energies on petitioning Virginia's legislature. His persistence and the results of his efforts speak both to the remarkable man that he was and to the simultaneous weight and changeableness of race.

CHAPTER THREE

petitioning for freedom
in an era of slavery

FOR A WHILE SAMUEL JOHNSON COULD ACCEPT that he held his family as his slaves—but only for a while. As he aged, he worried more and more about it. Johnson knew that their legal status held great importance even if Warrenton's residents and federal Census takers viewed his entire family as free. He knew that slave property, like any other property, could be seized to pay an outstanding debt, and he knew that the same was true if he waited to free his family in his will. If, for instance, he died owing more than could be paid by selling his other property, then his enslaved family would have to be sold to pay the debts; any emancipating provision would not take effect. What weighed most heavily upon him was probably less the issue of debt than his family's legal right to remain in Virginia. If he had only wanted to make them free, Johnson could simply have called upon one of the many people he knew who was familiar with the law and asked him to draft deeds of manumission for Patty, Sam Jr., and Lucy. What stopped Johnson was his keen attentiveness to the law and to doing things in a proper, socially accepted way. More than most free black Virginians, and probably more than most people, Samuel Johnson yearned for legitimacy—a socially and legally secure place for his family and himself in his homeland of Virginia.[1]

The quest for a legitimate place in Virginia had inspired his 1815 petition, and after its rejection he might have chosen to find a home with his family elsewhere. Pennsylvania was not so far away, and the family could all live freely there. But that is not the choice Johnson and his family made. From a modern perspective, it is difficult to understand their decision to stay in a slave state where they remained vulnerable rather than leave for a free state where they could all be secure in their liberty. Perhaps our difficulty in comprehending the Johnsons' decision lies in the fact that we tend to see freedom and slavery in binary terms, as opposites.

Samuel Johnson understood differently. He knew that the relationships he had built up in his community afforded him certain liberties, and that if he left his position at the tavern in Warrenton, he would not be able to replicate his special place at the center of the local community. He must have worried about how a man in his forties could build new connections and gain the respect and support of a new community. Would the white people elsewhere be as good to him as those in Warrenton? Would they support his dreams, declare that they wished him to live among them, write letters on his behalf to state senators? Would he gain the attention and aid of powerful political players? It did not seem likely, especially if Johnson considered, as he must have done, that even in free states black people often could not act as equals to whites. Furthermore, his was not a risk-taker's personality, and by contemporary standards he was getting old. Fauquier County was his home, and he wished to stay there with his family.

The simplest way to accomplish that was to free his family, and then they could remain together in Virginia in violation of the law. Johnson had considered that possibility when he had obtained his own freedom, and in the years since he had seen that officials hardly ever enforced the 1806 emigration law—another way in which white Virginians' behavior diverged from the ideals they wrote into law. Fauquier County delegate Thomas Marshall, son of Chief Justice John Marshall, said as much on the floor of the House of Delegates in 1832, noting that the 1806 law had "never been carried into effect" because "its provisions were in violation of the feelings of the people."[2] But "never" was not quite accurate. Every now and again an energetic local official determined to round up the illegal free black residents and sell them at auction, as the law provided, with the proceeds going to the Literary Fund of the state. (The Literary Fund provided monies to educate poor white Virginians, so free blacks' freedom fell sacrifice to the needs of the white poor.)[3]

How unlucky it was for Jack Bagwell in Accomack County, for example, when that county's overseers of the poor decided in 1825 to enforce the law they had long ignored. They arrested him, jailed him, and prepared to sell him. A friend paid his jail fee and Bagwell managed to escape from Virginia, but eight other free black Accomack County residents were not so lucky. When Bagwell's arrest failed to scare them into leaving, the overseers of the poor rounded them up and sold them as slaves.[4] A similar incident took place in Loudoun County, not far from Fauquier, when the commonwealth's attorney there decided in the 1830s to rid the county of its illegal free black population.[5] And poor George Jackson of Frederick County was sold back into slavery in 1833.[6]

Though this vigor in enforcing the 1806 provision dates from the period after Johnson first started petitioning, he knew enough of white Virginia's culture, had enough lawyers as friends, and was a visible enough figure in town that he wanted to avoid illegal residence. And he was, as we have seen, a by-the-book sort of person. He would not take the risk of seeing his family sold away after all those years of working to bring them together to freedom. Johnson held out hope that the legislature might act differently than it had in response to his 1815 petition and that it might yet grant Patty, Lucy, and Sam Jr. the same privilege it had granted him. Having decided not to ask the county court for permission for his family to remain in Virginia—a course of action that left no options if it failed—Johnson turned again to Virginia's lawmakers.

Johnson acted within a long Anglo-American tradition of petitioning that allowed people of marginal status to appeal to society's leaders. When enslaved blacks in the Boston area sought freedom in the era of the American Revolution, one of their tools was the petition. In his own era in Virginia, Johnson was joined by white Virginians petitioning the legislature for a wide range of abilities. They wanted to be allowed to dredge rivers, to move polling places, to get a divorce. Many black Virginians also petitioned the legislature, often for the same favor Johnson wanted: permission to remain in Virginia.[7]

Samuel Johnson's petitions reflected what he had learned from day-to-day life in Warrenton: race did not have to determine everything about a person's life or friendships, and a man like Johnson could find a welcome place in a community dominated by white people. The legislature's responses to his petitions demonstrated, by contrast, that lawmakers understood their duty to lie in reinscribing the racial lines that their society had agreed upon. Their sense of this duty to police Virginia's racial boundaries changed subtly but significantly over time.

By 1820 Johnson must have felt able to provide a more compelling case to the legislators than he had done in 1815, when they had tabled his first petition on his family's behalf. He now owned land and a house and was the most prominent of Warrenton's free black residents. As an increasingly established member of the community, he could reasonably hope that he might now be able to gain for Patty and the children permission to remain in Virginia if freed.

His third petition to the Virginia House of Delegates arose from that hope. Written in a hand different from those on his 1811 and 1815 petitions—a third person who helped—it began like the 1815 one, reminding the legislature that a number of years earlier it had authorized the emancipation of Samuel Johnson (here spelled Johnston) "upon the accommodation of divers respectable citizens . . . and in consideration of faithful services and singular good conduct." Since the time of his emancipation, his behavior "has been uniformly upright, industrious, & moral," and by "honest exertions, he has accumilated [*sic*], a tolerable estate, consisting of real and personal property." The point was not only that Johnson posed no threat to the community, but that he was part of it and exemplified the qualities and achievements that the society endorsed and encouraged: good moral conduct and material success. He seemed to expect that these achievements in themselves deserved reward according to an implicit social contract: if a man behaved according to society's rules, he would be rewarded with status, power, and personal freedom. (Society rewarded well-behaved women somewhat differently, with respect instead of power, and with feminine honor instead of personal freedom.) Johnson's petition asserted, although not in so many words, that what one did ought to matter more than the color of one's skin. Samuel Johnson thought that meeting the dominant standards of propriety would erase distinctions of color.[8]

To demonstrate how little color mattered, Johnson had to show the legislators that his family members were also upright and moral community members. The petition stated that Johnson and the "said slaves" had all conducted themselves in such a way as to meet "with the approbation of all the most sober and prudent part of the community." Calling his family "slaves" undercut the implicit argument that color should not matter, but the thirty-eight white people (the same number, though not all the same people, as in 1811) who signed his petition helped again to diminish the social distinctions that race normally marked. In endorsing the petition as factually correct and joining "in soliciting the passage of the act prayed for in the petition," they demonstrated the strong ties that could exist between free people of different "races." They suggested that a community of free people might act together.

In this way, the petition of 1820 inaugurated a strategy Johnson and his scribes would employ in later petitions. The authors—Johnson and whoever helped him—worked hard to create a feeling of sympathy between the legislators and Johnson by portraying him as someone just like them, only with darker skin. They tried to erase race even as the petition's very existence, the necessity for a black man to request to keep his family with him in freedom, reminded the legislators of Virginia's legally inscribed racial divisions. The petition stated that it was "from feelings incidental to all men" (I am a man like you) that he wanted to free his family. It was also from feelings "peculiar to those individuals who have led the harmless and unexceptionable life of your petitioner" (You need not fear me). The petition also asked for sympathy by portraying Johnson's dilemma. He would "long ago have executed a Deed of emancipation had he not been intimidated by the penalties of the Statute which requires their speedy departure from the Commonwealth" (I am law abiding). Finally, Johnson and his scribe appealed to the hearts of their readers. "Your petitioner therefore humbly seeks from your honourable body" the requested dispensation "by which your petitioner in his declining years will be secured in the enjoyment of those natural blessings, and domestic comforts, to which from his long and faithful services as well as his virtuous course of life he trusts he is entitled." (I am old, I have worked hard, do I not deserve the comforts of family as I approach death?)

To further bolster his case, and because one of the issues in freeing any slave was monetary, Johnson also stated some cold facts concerning his wealth. He appended to his petition a statement signed by three white men who attested to the value of his property. Johnson needed to demonstrate that emancipating his family would not defraud creditors and also that he could support his family so that they would not become a burden to the community. The estimated worth of his estate (including the value of Patty, Lucy, and Sam Jr., presumably) was a surprisingly large thirty-six hundred dollars. This impressive sum supported his claim of being industrious, but it leaves us with a mystery. His house and land were worth several hundred dollars, and his slaves, including perhaps the older man living in his household, probably not more than a thousand dollars. What can account for the additional two thousand dollars? The tax records of those years do not indicate that property values had risen dramatically. Instead, after the financial panic of 1819, property values generally declined. Perhaps he owned a horse already in 1820, since records show that he owned one in 1827.[9] But it could not have been worth two thousand dollars. Perhaps the assessors were simply being generous? Perhaps it was fraud? No answer fully satisfies.

Although how Johnson could have amassed an estate worth thirty-six hundred dollars, or whether the assessment was at all truthful, remains unknown, it is clear that the strong combination of strategies employed in his 1820 petition almost worked. After the petition was referred, as a matter of course, to the Committee on the Courts of Justice, the members decided that "so much as [he] prays that his wife be permitted to remain in this Common'th, is reasonable." But they "rejected" the request that Lucy and Sam Jr. be allowed to remain. Consequently, they drew up a bill allowing Patty, but not the children, to remain in Virginia if freed. What the legislators presumably had in mind with such a move was to extend some favor to Johnson by allowing his wife to be freed, but to ensure that his descendants would not add to what white Virginians perceived as a threatening population of free blacks. Thus the legislators' judgment on the question of race was that it *did* matter—quite a lot. As distant observers rather than neighbors and acquaintances of the Johnson family, and acting in their capacity as legislators and not as friends, they were more inclined to implement the law than to make exceptions to it, and more inclined to build up race than to see beyond it.

The half measure they approved died, however, without the aid of someone like John Scott to see it through to passage. The bill allowing Patty to remain never became law because it was never read aloud in the House of Delegates the required three times and never received the approbation of the delegates. It was not an unusual fate for a bill; Virginia's legislature typified others then and now, passing only a portion of the many bills it considered. But even if it had become law, it would have been insufficient in Samuel Johnson's eyes. Why would he and Patty want to stay in Virginia if young Sam and Lucy had to go? The family would have to soldier on as they had, living between slavery and freedom.

Johnson proceeded to further build his family's life. It was after the rejection of his third petition that he bought from his neighbors John A. W. and Maria L. Smith a half acre of land adjacent to the plot he already owned. As he would later indicate, this land served as an investment; buying real estate was a sound and conservative way to store and manage wealth. The land might also, in the future when his children married, serve as the site of new houses for their families. In the meantime, the Johnsons could use the land, if they wished, as a garden, raising produce such as corn and vegetables to supplement their diet. What is clear is that in spite of the recent failure, Samuel Johnson had no intention of giving up on any of his dreams: to become materially successful and to be able to pass his wealth to his children, who would be free and allowed to remain in Virginia.

Soon, however, tragedy struck at those dreams. Sam Jr. was somehow, cruelly, taken away—illness, accident, we do not know. He simply disappeared. A petition written a couple of years later mentioned his death obliquely, saying that "at this time [Johnson] has no other child" than Lucy. The phrase indicated that there had once been another child, and that the other child's absence was permanent. The very fact of our not knowing what happened to young Sam, who was probably in his late teens at the time, speaks volumes about the status of free blacks and about the role of government in the early nation. Today, states mandate that local governments issue death certificates and that each death be recorded and given a cause. In early nineteenth-century Virginia, people buried and mourned their dead without such government intervention, so there is no public record of young Sam's demise. And because Johnson was illiterate, there are no letters or diaries that might have survived to tell us of Sam Jr.'s fate. Local newspapers would not have taken account of the death of a young slave, even if his father worked in the tavern. Not listed in the records of Warrenton's cemetery, his name not recorded in compilations of local gravestone inscriptions made by twentieth-century genealogists, young Samuel Johnson Jr. simply ceased to be. Dust to dust.[10]

We can only imagine the family's grief, the debilitating sense of loss. Johnson had wanted to pass on his line. He had, in a clear assertion of paternal pride and responsibility, named his son after himself. Sam Jr. was to be his heir. The death of a child, and the dreams crushed by that death, would cause some people to retreat, to stop trying so hard, and to focus instead on surviving day to day, grateful for what was left. But not Samuel Johnson. He was not one to give up in the face of tragedy. It only made him more determined to ensure Lucy's future. With impressive, even unreasonable, optimism, he continued to hope and work for the best.

Word had come that he had not provided sufficient proof in his latest petition of "his strong and peculiar claims." The terms of the law specified that general merit was insufficient, and that applicants for permission to remain in Virginia as exceptions to the 1806 statute had to demonstrate that they had performed specific meritorious acts.[11] Since the legislators had not found that his request had merit above and beyond similar requests from others, he would try again, with more ammunition this time, to make his request stand out.

He would also refocus his efforts. It did not matter so much whether Patty were freed; she was past childbearing age so would not give birth to any more enslaved children. She was also not as likely as Lucy to outlive Samuel Johnson. With Sam Jr. gone, Johnson's main concern became Lucy, who would someday have children of her own, children who would all be slaves if she were not legally freed.

A fourth petition, 1822: "Your petitioner having now furnished himself additional evidence to support" the previous petition "humbly prayeth that your honours will reconsider his aforesaid [1820] application." Someone signed Johnson's name for him, and three others signed the main petition as well. Again there was a testimonial, signed by forty-two of the town's white men. They attested that they had "long been acquainted with Samuel Johnston the petitioner a free man of colour." They knew his "character & deportment" and found him "unusually correct & upright as to entitle him to singular public favour." They joined him in asking the legislature to grant his request. A note also came from the tavern, now Thompson's, stating that its owner, James Horner, had known Johnson a decade or more. Horner declared Johnson to be "a very honest industrious man"—not a boy, not a man of color, and not a colored man, but simply a "man." Moreover, Horner said, Johnson had been "attentive and obliging."[12]

What is particularly interesting about the strategy employed in the 1822 petition is that Lucy's freedom depended less on evidence of her own good behavior, honesty, loyalty, and industry than on her father's. As a female person of color she was doubly debilitated, doubly restricted from the world of freedom, power, independence. In a time when even white women were under the law considered more as their husband's property than as independent agents, Lucy, a slave girl, hardly appeared as an individual in the petition written on her behalf.[13] Granting her a right to remain in Virginia was understood to be a favor done for her father—both free and male, a "man" even in some white people's eyes—and not a favor for Lucy herself.

This petition was, like the others, referred to the Committee on the Courts of Justice. And although the assertion that Johnson's conduct had been "so unusually correct & upright as to entitle him to singular public favour" did not demonstrate an "act or acts of extraordinary merit" as the law required, the committee—wondrous!—found Johnson's petition reasonable.[14] On the day before Christmas, December 24, 1822, a bill was drawn up that would grant Lucy the right to remain in Virginia if freed by her father.

It looked as if Samuel Johnson had finally achieved what he had so long sought. It had been a full decade since he had walked out of the courthouse and into his own freedom. Now it appeared that his descendants, through Lucy, would be able to live as free people, too.

Alas, the bill drawn up in response to Johnson's 1822 petition, like the previous bill, failed to become law; it was not read aloud the required number of times to be passed by the House of Delegates and never made it to the Virginia Senate for concurrence. What might have been the happiest new year ever instead opened as another year of challenges. Rather than give up, however, the Johnsons found that the near-success of 1822 made them all the more determined.

Another consideration pushed them to keep petitioning. In the early 1820s Lucy was nearing marriageable age. She would soon have suitors, young African American men who would, no doubt, see her as an attractive mate, especially because her father was so relatively well-off and would be able to help the young couple get settled. If Lucy were a free woman and married a free man, she would be the first in her family to be legally wed. The issues surrounding courtship would be different for her than they had been for her enslaved mother, who had no property to offer her spouse and no paternal assistance.

But Lucy could not get legally and properly married and could not have free children unless her father emancipated her. Propriety was important to Samuel Johnson, so rather than try to skirt the law or marry Lucy off without the state's recognition, Johnson in 1823 sent another petition to the legislature, his fifth in just over a decade and his third in four years. This time, he asked for permission to free both Patty and Lucy.

The 1823 petition broke a bit from the formula employed in his previous petitions. It did not mention the kindness the legislature had bestowed to Samuel Johnson in 1812. But it did establish in the first sentence that Johnson was a man of "industry & faithful services," living a "life of activity and honesty" by which he had purchased his own freedom and acquired his wife and daughter (the dead son not mentioned) as his slaves. Understanding the objections white Virginians had to allowing free blacks in Virginia, understanding that they feared the increase of this anomalous population that was neither slave nor white, Johnson's fifth petition emphasized how little his family would add to that population: "his wife from her advanced age can bear no more [children]." He did not mention Lucy's growing maturity. Rather, he emphasized that Patty and Lucy pursued "the habits & course of life" that "recommend them to the favour & good opinion of all the citizens of this county who know them." Not only were they people who could form no threat, their neighbors valued and appreciated them. Furthermore, they would not become a financial burden to the community because Samuel Johnson had "acquired comfortable real estate for their maintenance." When he died, that little bit of property would keep them out of poverty, away from the responsibilities of the overseers of the poor, who distributed cash relief to poor residents or bound out poor children and orphans as apprentices.[15]

Johnson's worries and sense of justice come through once again. He was, the petition said, "anxious and desirous to have them freed with liberty to remain in the county of Fauquier."

"[H]e thinks the exemplary conduct of himself & his wife & daughter entitles them to the kindness of your honourable body." Surely, he implied, if a person follows the rules, succeeds beyond all expectations, rises from slavery to become a man of property and respect, he deserves some reward, not as a favor but as his due. He earned it. And yet the form of the petition required him to approach as a supplicant: "He therefore prays that an act may be passed to authorize the emancipation & permanent residence in Fauquier County of his said wife & daughter."[16]

The testimonial accompanying the 1823 petition affirmed its contents to be true and demonstrated that numerous people joined Johnson in his request. There were more names on this testimonial than any of the previous ones—eighty-seven, including that of the former state senator John Scott, who also served for years as commonwealth's attorney for Fauquier County. Scott signed at the top, in the right-hand column, and wrote, "I am acquainted with the within named petitioner and believe the facts set forth herein are true." Other wealthy and important members of the community put their names on it too: Johnson's neighbor the court clerk John A. W. Smith; James Horner, the owner of the tavern; Thomas Thornton Withers, a local doctor; Alexander Marshall, the chief justice's nephew; and M. A. Chilton, who taught school, held a large number of slaves (twenty-five in 1830), and was a few years later elected to represent Fauquier County in the state legislature.[17] Even Richard Chichester, who had a violent relationship with black people, supported Johnson's petition. He was another local notable whose name appears frequently in the county records, and he was twice arraigned for murdering slaves he owned, one a woman named Rachel and the other a man named Joshua. Both times the court, including Samuel Johnson's former owner, the "gentleman justice" Edward Digges, found that there was not enough evidence to bring him to trial. Chichester's reputation seems to have survived intact. Despite the fact that two of his slaves died under his care, he was still asked to sign a petition in favor of a black family.[18]

Again the petition was found reasonable; again a bill was drawn up; again the bill failed to become law.

How could he give up now? So, a sixth petition, 1824. This one began with the reminder that the legislature had passed an act for "*his emancipation* in the year of ———." The blank space suggested that Johnson could not remember the year of his emancipation, perhaps did not think in years, and had not brought his records to the man who wrote this petition. The petition's author was yet a new writer, as it appeared in a different hand. Perhaps Johnson did not want to burden the same people over again with his requests to draft a petition, or maybe he figured that if the previous writer had failed, he should try someone new.

The similarities between the petitions seem, then, to have sprung from Johnson's similar conversations with his scribes. If, for instance, the man who wrote the 1824 petition had seen a copy of the 1823 one, he would not have left blank the year in which Samuel Johnson was emancipated, since the 1823 petition had included that information. Otherwise, the 1823 and 1824 petitions had much in common, containing similar information and similarly expressing Johnson's concern and anguish. The 1824 petition ended with another appeal to the emotions: "Your petitioner therefore hoping that his ardent pursuit of an object to him most important and most dear, will not be offensive to your honorable body, humbly requests that an act of your honorable body may be passed."[19]

Once more, Johnson managed to get many of his acquaintances to sign his request. Edward Digges supported him, and a number of people whose names had been on the previous year's petition signed again. The total this time was more modest but still impressive, if you consider how unlikely it was that a free black man, a member of a community so despised, could persuade his neighbors to support his request to remain with his family among them. There were fifty names this time. One of the members of the legislature, perhaps the clerk, counted them, indicating that the number was important; at the bottom of the petition, the number "50" is written. Personalized notes from John Shackelford and J. C. Gibson bolstered the petition. The notes said that they knew Samuel Johnson as a man of "good character" (Shackelford) and as a "faithfull servant" (Gibson). Shackelford's handwriting strongly resembles that on the petition itself, and he may have been its writer.[20]

Since a number of legislators served in the House of Delegates for several years in a row and sat repeatedly on committees such as the Committee on the Courts of Justice, at least a few of them were by now familiar with Samuel Johnson of Fauquier County and his requests. Johnson must have hoped to wear them down with his persistence. In 1824 they rejected his petition, but there are markings on the back that indicate that the legislature reconsidered the request in 1825. That year, they found the petition reasonable and drew up a bill in accord. Patty and Lucy would be allowed to remain, but only in Fauquier County. This 1825 bill, like the previous ones, failed to become law.[21]

Incapable of giving up, Johnson sent another petition to the legislature the next year, in 1826, the fifth in six years. Samuel Johnson had to be the most dogged individual to come to the legislature's attention in the whole of antebellum Virginia. No one else sent so many petitions asking for the same thing. No one else took rejection so lightly. It must have been almost comical to some of the more hard-hearted committee members, to see different versions of the same request arrive on their desk year after year.[22]

Samuel, Patty, and Lucy would have found little comedy in the matter. All those mentions of Johnson's "anxious" desire and of his entitlement to favor bespoke someone who viewed the issue with great seriousness. Like a caged creature who could see the hole for his escape but not fit his body through until the hole was made just the tiniest bit larger, Johnson would keep pushing.

In 1826 Samuel Johnson had a special reason not to give up: Lucy was that year engaged to be married to a young free black man named Spencer Malvin. She was twenty-one years old and Spencer was twenty-two. The year before, Malvin had registered with the county clerk, who recorded in the Register of Free Negroes that he was 5 feet 8½ inches tall, a "Mulatto Man" with "short bushy hair" who had been "Born free." Being free-born meant that in contrast to Samuel Johnson, Spencer Malvin knew his birthday, February 12, 1804, the same date on which Abraham Lincoln was born five years later.[23]

Malvin was a man of some skills, a "thriving intelligent mechanic," carpenter, and laborer.[24] He was also literate. Though his spelling was poor ("bot" for bought, "hors" for horse), he could scratch out an intelligible note and keep his own business records.[25] Perhaps most important, Malvin had a strong sense of his own person. He knew how to stand up for himself, which his behavior as an adolescent demonstrated.

In 1818 the fourteen-year-old Spencer Malvin had been working as an apprentice to one Fielding Sinclair when Sinclair killed his "negro boy Slave named Charles." Malvin had likely witnessed the horrifying event—very little was private or secret in antebellum Virginia. Sinclair was charged with murder, implying that at least some white people thought that he had gone beyond the normal violence one could legally inflict on one's slave property. But Spencer Malvin could not share what he might have seen because black people could not testify against white ones. The judges found insufficient evidence to hold Sinclair for trial, and the case was dismissed. Perhaps because of his own inability to testify in court, Malvin faced living with a man who had killed someone much like himself—a young, male, Afro-Virginian worker in his household.[26]

Malvin wanted to get away from Sinclair—to get away from the trauma as well as to make sure that he did not suffer the same fate as the poor dead Charles. As a bound apprentice, Malvin could not leave without the court's permission, which he sought a month after Sinclair's release. He went to court and asked for an annulment of his apprenticeship contract on the grounds of "Misusage." The court had great sympathy with him, not only placing the burden of proof on Sinclair to show why Malvin should not be released, but in the meantime placing Malvin under the care of the overseers of the poor. Since Malvin was not returned to his parents, it seems that either his father was not alive or that his father was considered to be too impoverished to provide for him. When Sinclair appeared in court the following month, the court sided with Spencer Malvin and revoked the apprenticeship. The overseers of the poor subsequently bound him out as an apprentice to a tanner, but apparently he pushed for something else, for a few months later he was bound out again, this time to be a "Homejoiner & carpenter."[27]

As there were few eligible free black men in town, or even in the county, Lucy probably felt lucky to be the object of Malvin's attention. She was probably attracted to his dignity and toughness as well as his practical skills and ability to provide for her. Likewise Malvin, who had a bit of a rough adolescence, probably felt that he had done well to secure the hand of the daughter of Samuel Johnson, a stable and dignified man who might become a father figure to him. No longer an abstract possibility, Lucy's impending marriage made the matter of her freedom all the more important.

Johnson finally decided he had to emancipate her. On the same day in late September 1826 that Lucy and Spencer filed the paperwork indicating their intention to wed, Johnson oversaw the drafting of a deed of manumission that would free Lucy. It stated, "I, Samuel Johnston, . . . for and in consideration of the natural love and affection which I bear to my daughter Lucy Johnston . . .

who is my slave, do hereby emancipate manumit & set free my said daughter Lucy Johnston & do hereby release & relinquish & convey to her all right which I may have to her personal services." As Richard Brent had done fourteen years earlier for Samuel, now Samuel did for Lucy: he gave her legal rights over her own self. Johnson signed the document with his mark, an X. Later, the county clerk, their neighbor John A. W. Smith, would copy the deed into the official records and deliver the original back to Lucy so that she would have proof of her liberty.[28]

Once she was free, the wedding could go on. On September 27, 1826, a Wednesday, Lucy Johnson and Spencer Malvin were married by the Reverend Richard H. Barnes, who remains an obscure figure.[29] Later records indicate that the wedding was held in a church. Knowing what we do about Samuel Johnson, we can surmise that it was a respectable affair, with a small celebration afterward. There would be no jumping over broomsticks, no reminders of the slave past.

Now free, Lucy could not remain legally in Virginia beyond September 26, 1827. Johnson knew that any additional pleas to the legislature on her behalf would have to top his previous efforts, which had come close to success but had never achieved it. Rather than change tactics, however, Johnson simply did more of what had led to near-success in the past.

His seventh petition did not differ much from the others, although it was better written and mentioned only Lucy, not Patty. It contained concise prose that borrowed heavily from the previous petitions, suggesting that Johnson had kept copies of at least some of them and brought them to his latest scribe, and also reflecting the fact that by 1826 enough free blacks had asked for such favor that petitions to remain in Virginia possessed a certain formulaic quality. But again, Johnson did not carry to his scribe anything that showed the year in which he had been emancipated, for that information was once more left blank.

Probably because Johnson wanted to obscure the fact, the 1826 petition did not mention that he had already emancipated Lucy. It said that "your petitioner has . . . acquired the ownership of his daughter Lucy, that the upright deportment and good moral character of said Lucy has acquired for her the favour respect and good wishes of the community generally, that your petitioner with those feelings natural to men whose lives are not blemished with vice or crime possesses an anxious desire that his daughter should be free and reside in the land of her nativity where he has realized property sufficient for her support." He ended, as usual, with an appeal to sympathy, that his "ardent pursuit of an object to him most important and most dear will not be offensive to your Honourable Body."[30]

As concisely argued as it was, the petition would, Johnson knew, fail on its own. Johnson did more. He arranged for a notice to be posted on the front door of the courthouse declaring his intention to submit a petition to the General Assembly asking that his daughter, Lucy Malvin, whom he had emancipated, be allowed to remain in Virginia. The courthouse poster, even if it did not say it in so many words, served also as notice that others could sign the petition. In consequence, more people than ever before joined in Johnson's request, 226 individuals. For the first time the signers included several women, notably Ann Norris, who had raised Lucy in her house, and Sarah D. Digges, the daughter of Johnson's long-ago owner Edward Digges.[31]

In addition, Johnson's supporters in 1826 included two prominent members of an important and politically influential Virginia family, the Barbours. Once again, Johnson's access to Virginia's movers and shakers, as well as his own winning personality, helped him engage powerful help. John Strode Barbour of neighboring Culpeper County was a sitting U.S. congressman who described Johnson as "one of the most worthy & reputable free persons of colour that I have ever known. His good conduct has secured to him the kind wishes of every person to whom he is known. I unite very cordially in the prayer of his petition." Around 1820 Barbour had practiced law in Warrenton and, most likely, had then gotten to know Samuel Johnson. He thought so highly of Johnson that he seems to have talked his cousin Philip Pendleton Barbour into signing too, for their handwritten testimonials appeared together on the same sheet of paper. Philip Pendleton Barbour had also served in Congress, as the Speaker of the House in the 1821–22 session. In 1826 he was a judge on the Virginia General Court, and having in September "*yielded* to the solicitations of the Freeholders to become a candidate for Congress," was shortly to return to the national capital to represent Virginia. (In addition, Philip's brother James was then serving as secretary of war.) This renowned and surely very busy Virginia leader found time to support Johnson's request and to write, in his own hand, "From the information of others on whom I can rely, I consider the petitioner, a man of good character & conduct and highly meritorious."[32]

It is worth emphasizing that neither Barbour was an enemy to slavery. Both owned tens of slaves (though Philip was much richer), and both voted against a congressional resolution to consider abolishing slavery in the District of Columbia.[33] As we have seen, people behaved differently when confronted with individuals standing before them than when considering slaves or free blacks as abstractions; and granting favor to a well-deserving free man of color made the whole social system, with its entrenched and legally recognized categories and hierarchies, appear more just.

The 1826 petition was extraordinary, on the face of it superior even to the petition of 1811 by which Samuel Johnson had succeeded in obtaining permission to remain in Virginia. He had on his side hundreds of white men and women and two U.S. congressmen, one of whom was a sitting judge on Virginia's General Court. But perhaps the members of the Committee on the Courts of Justice realized that, since Johnson's daughter's name

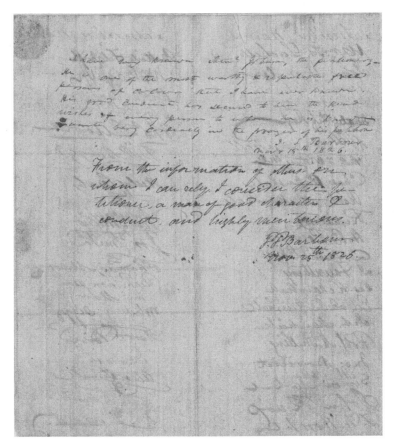

John Strode Barbour's and Philip Pendleton Barbour's notes endorsing Samuel Johnson's 1826 petition. The Barbours wrote on the back of the first page of subscribers' names, which are partially visible in this image. SJP 1826.

was now Lucy Malvin, a fact mentioned not in the petition's main text but in the appended copy of the courthouse notice, she had married and would likely soon give birth to free black children. Adding to the free black population was precisely what white Virginians had hoped to prevent when twenty years before they had passed the law dictating that freed slaves would have to leave Virginia. Further, the Barbours' notes, like similar notes in previous petitions, had attested to Samuel's worthiness but not Lucy's. Allowing her to remain would be a favor to him, but she no longer carried his name and presumably did not reside in his house, and there was little evidence that she would provide enough of a benefit to the community to make an exception to the 1806 law. In general, men had better claims than women did to their worth in the community. It was men who did the jobs society valued and who contributed to the economy and the community in visible ways. Women's work, while crucial, did not earn them similar status, partly because they performed it behind closed doors in the home. Her father might have been a beloved and key member of the community, but Lucy Malvin was in the minds of the white legislators merely a colored woman, the wife of a black man who remained anonymous to them, and a potential procreator of unwanted "free negro" babies.

This time, there was not even a bill drawn in response. The petition, even with its several pages of endorsements, was simply rejected, which left Lucy in a precarious position. Although it was unlikely in a community so friendly to Samuel Johnson that anyone would enforce the law that required her to go, it was still possible that if she stayed more than the allotted twelve months she could be taken by the county overseers of the poor and sold at auction.[34]

Lucy did not leave Virginia. Neither did she flaunt her freedom. Unlike her father and her new husband, she never registered as a "free negro."[35] She and her father also hid her status in subsequent legal papers. None of the documents or later petitions that were filed during Samuel Johnson's lifetime describes her as free. In spite of the deed of manumission, and also because of it, her legal status seemed in doubt. Spencer Malvin must have known that his new wife might at some point have to leave the state to avoid being sold, but he did not then suggest that they depart.

And so life went on, but not without an eighth attempt to sway the legislature, this one a request to allow both Patty and

Lucy to remain. The petition again framed the request as a favor due to Samuel, and mentioned nothing of Lucy's marriage or her status as a free woman. With fewer names attached than before and no new evidence to offer of Lucy's and Patty's worth, the 1828 petition was, like the previous one, rejected outright.[36]

The rejection of the 1826 and 1828 petitions reflected a growing antipathy among white Virginians, a hardening of attitudes toward African Americans and their efforts to be free. Earlier in the century, many of Virginia's judges had ruled in favor of African American plaintiffs in lawsuits requesting freedom. The judicial authorities in Virginia had believed that liberty had great value and should be restricted only in clear-cut cases. In 1804, for instance, they granted freedom to the slaves of Quaker Gloister Hunnicutt, whose 1781 emancipation of them predated the 1782 manumission law. One of the judges ruling in favor of the blacks' freedom explained, "Devises in favour . . . of liberty, ought to be liberally expounded."[37] In addition, lawmakers, as we have seen, sometimes wrote legislation on behalf of black petitioners like Samuel Johnson.

The Missouri Crisis and Compromise of 1819–21 helped to change white Virginians' attitudes. The first major eruption of that conflict occurred when New York congressman James Tallmadge proposed in 1819 that the territory of Missouri be admitted as a state only if slavery were banned from Missouri in the future. The debate that followed proved highly sectional, and congressmen voted more by region — North versus South — than by party affiliation. Philip Pendleton Barbour, who would sign Johnson's 1826 petition, owed his prominence in good measure to the states' rights arguments he helped develop in 1819–20. In the congressional debates, Barbour asserted that states alone, and not the federal government, had the power to determine the status of slavery within their borders. Along with all the other Virginia congressmen, he voted against the ban on future slavery in Missouri. Barbour also rejected the eventual compromise line of 36°30', the latitude above which slavery would in future be barred from western territories. Feeling attacked from without, Barbour and Virginia's other leaders moved more firmly and clearly into the proslavery camp in just a couple of intensely political years.[38]

After the Missouri Compromise, the newly strengthened imperative to protect slavery affected how Virginia's judges acted and how ordinary white Virginians perceived their relationship to slavery. In lawsuits, judges began to rule against African American plaintiffs on mere technicalities they had ignored before.[39] In newspaper editorials and public discussions, white Virginians stood together to oppose verbal attacks on slavery that came increasingly from the North.[40]

Attacks on slavery took more physical form too. In 1822 Denmark Vesey, a free black man in Charleston, South Carolina, planned a massive rebellion and exodus of slaves. Although it failed, the plot was discussed widely in Virginia's newspapers.[41] In 1826 white Virginians could sympathize, and feel horrified, when they read in the newspaper about the "Virginia gentleman" who "had his nose broke" in a "riot" in New York City. The "riot" had erupted after the city magistrates there decided to allow a black family to be taken by the Virginians who claimed them as slaves.[42]

The growth of the domestic slave trade, like the 1826 New York "riot," focused Americans' attentions on the issue of slaves who crossed state lines. Virginia participated extensively in the domestic slave trade, supplying thousands of slaves to the new plantations of the deep South. Slavery had become an issue of national political significance.

Although white Virginians had not needed to defend slavery very vigorously during the Revolutionary era, in part because a number of Virginia's leaders projected a theoretical antislavery stance, white Virginians in the 1820s felt that they did. They faced an increasingly multifaceted and broad attack on the institution at the center of their culture and economy (which now included selling slaves out of state). In the 1820s they began to understand that defending slavery required defending the whole entangled thing: race and slavery together as a way of organizing society, not just slavery as a system of labor. Samuel Johnson and his family were some of the victims of this rededication to enforcing Virginia's racial rules.

The death of Thomas Jefferson on July 4, 1826 (the fiftieth anniversary of the Declaration of Independence, and the same day that John Adams died) symbolized this transformation, the passing of the Revolutionary age. That was the same year that Lucy announced her intent to wed Spencer Malvin and that Samuel Johnson emancipated her. By then, liberty, for which the American Revolution had been fought, meant something narrower and more practical than it had in the idealistic age into which Johnson had been born. It was more apparent now than it had been throughout the previous half century that freedom in America was white.

CHAPTER FOUR

visions of rebellion

PERHAPS NAT TURNER WAS RESPONDING partly to the greater restrictions on liberty in Virginia when he plotted what became the most famous and most deadly slave rebellion in American history. In late August 1831 Turner, a literate and deeply religious slave also known as Preacher Nat, led a group of rebels from farm to farm in Virginia's Southampton County, near the North Carolina border. They killed all the white people—men, women, and children—they could find. Turner and his followers hoped their actions would generate a great uprising of slaves that would end white dominance and fulfill Turner's vision that "the first should be last and the last should be first."[1] Nat Turner's stated goal of racial inversion—black over white—was precisely what white Virginians most feared. In calling forth a picture of an alternate reality in which all black people might be truly free, Turner's Rebellion destroyed white complacency about slavery and gave black people cause to reexamine their place in the world. For the Johnson-Malvin family, the rebellion, its aftermath, and its consequences would rock their lives and rattle the family they had determined to keep together. For worse and not for better, Turner's Rebellion altered the landscape in which they lived, as it altered the political landscape in all of Virginia and the nation beyond it.[2]

The earthquake of Turner's Rebellion struck all the harder because changes of the previous decade had already begun to shake things up. The Missouri Crisis and Compromise of 1819–21 had introduced a more intense version of the national political battle over slavery. Antislavery activists, both black and white, had begun organizing and publishing in the northern states. And the nation as a whole was undergoing massive economic and social change. Population statistics tell part of the story: the 5.3 million people who lived in the United States in 1800, when Samuel Johnson began planning his freedom, had grown nearly two and a half times to 12.9 million in 1830, the year before Turner's Rebellion.[3] Along with population growth came geographic expansion and the growth and elaboration of commercial markets. People at the time fretted over the rapid changes. As early as 1817, South Carolina politician John C. Calhoun expressed his concern that "we are . . . rapidly—I was about to say fearfully—growing." For Calhoun, national growth had centrifugal force—something to be fought against. The nation's swift development brought with it "the most imperious obligation to counteract every tendency to disunion."[4]

Samuel Johnson observed up close one of the ways in which Americans tried to counteract any tendency to disunion when Warrenton's residents hosted a grand, fiftieth-anniversary celebration of the nation's birth. In 1824–25, General Lafayette, the French aide to General Washington and a beloved hero of the American Revolution, made a triumphal and nostalgic visit to the United States. His tour launched a period of nationalistic festivities, building up to the fiftieth anniversary of the Declaration of Independence in 1826. Lafayette traveled to all twenty-four states, visiting Virginia twice. In late August 1825 he arrived in Fauquier County, where he was greeted with great ceremony—boys in uniform, men on horses, esteemed guests in carriages. In Warrenton he listened as Thomas L. Moore, who had witnessed Samuel Johnson's deed of emancipation, made a celebratory speech before a crowd of five or six thousand people. Afterward, Lafayette graciously responded, speaking of his love of Virginia and of republican principles.[5]

Surely Samuel Johnson worked among the servants who made the occasion possible, for the reception following Moore's speech took place in "Mrs. Norris's Tavern." (Ann Norris was now in charge.) A bit later, "under a handsome arbour in the beautiful green in front of the Tavern," "a large company sat down to a sumptuous and elegant dinner prepared by Mrs. Norris." Ann Norris's former charge Lucy Johnson Malvin probably helped to prepare and serve this feast to the guests, who included ex-president James Monroe and Chief Justice John Marshall. A couple of years earlier Monroe, as president of the United States, had issued the invitation for Lafayette to visit America. Now dining with the honored general, Monroe led the guests in raising their glasses to Lafayette. He toasted: "Neither time, nor titles, nor dungeons, have abated the love of the patriot for the liberty of nations." (Monroe referred to the time that Lafayette spent imprisoned during the French Revolution.) Lafayette rose and responded with a toast of his own to "the Old Virginia Line, the Militia of 1781, and the present generation of Fauquier: May the Revolutionary services of the fathers, find an everlasting reward in the Republican prosperity and happiness of their children."[6]

What thoughts crossed Samuel Johnson's mind as he heard slaveholders celebrate republican liberty? Monroe owned numerous slaves who worked his plantation, and had taken six with him to Washington when he served as president; John Marshall had seven slaves living in his Richmond home; and Thomas L. Moore owned three.[7] What did Johnson think when they toasted Jefferson, "the *Friend* of freedom" who, rumor had it, had fathered children with his slave mistress? Was he too busy to notice, occupied with seeing to the details of the day, serving food and drink, and watching over other servants? Or was he too inured to the ways of Virginia to notice the contrasts and ironies?

Unlike Monroe's and Lafayette's, Johnson's thoughts on the occasion did not make it into the newspapers. In contrast to John C. Calhoun, Samuel Johnson did not speechify in the halls of Congress, did not ever run for president, and appears not once in any history textbook.[8] Nat Turner's name became well known, but Samuel Johnson's did not. But as much as any of those more famous people, Johnson and his family had to navigate the changes of the 1820s and early 1830s. They had to decide how to respond to the events they witnessed and the alterations of attitude and practice they perceived. They had to reckon with history. In so doing, the Johnson-Malvin clan, like all of us, helped to make history.

One sign of the way in which the Johnson-Malvin family responded to the changes of the period was their decision to stop petitioning the legislature, at least for a while. Instead, they turned their attention to their daily lives together under Samuel Johnson's roof, where the extended family now lived. Lucy and Spencer began to have children. They named their first child, born about 1828, Sam, in honor of Lucy's beloved and esteemed father and in memory of her brother, Sam Jr. Because Samuel and Spencer could provide a stable income, Lucy was likely able to stay home with the baby, a privilege very few black women had. Together, she and her mother could care for little Sam, feeding and changing him, singing to him when he fussed, helping him to sleep. While the women busied themselves with the many tasks of running the household, the constant chores of cooking and cleaning, Samuel Johnson continued to work at the tavern. Spencer Malvin traveled about the county by horse to work as a mechanic, taking with him a cart and his carpenter's tools. He likely did a number of tasks: hauling goods, repairing and constructing buildings, and perhaps also repairing carriages, hanging doors, and the like.[9]

An 1830 statistical snapshot of the household shows that other people lived with the Johnson-Malvin family. The Census taker of that year recorded, in addition to Samuel, Patty, Spencer, Lucy, and the baby, two young people in the household. They were between ten and twenty-four years old and may have been boarders or hired help. If they were hired help, that put the family into the ranks of the middling classes; but even if they were boarders, that indicated that the house was fairly large and that the family had considerable resources. All of the people living under Samuel Johnson's roof in 1830 were listed as free blacks and not slaves, even Patty, whose legal status as a slave mattered less to the Census taker than her social status as a free man's wife, a woman who did not *appear* to be enslaved.[10] For the moment at least, the family's place between slavery and freedom — Patty's vulnerable position as a legal slave, and Lucy's illegal residence in Virginia — seemed not to matter.

But careful attention to current events would have caused Johnson concern that his family's in-between status mattered very much. Virginia politics in those years were heated, and at the center of the political discussions of the period lay topics deeply relevant to the family and especially to Samuel Johnson: freedom, equality, and manly participation in the community. Johnson could listen but not participate in these discussions, which culminated in the 1829–30 Virginia Constitutional Convention, where the issues of slavery and freedom took a prominent place. Political developments in the rest of the nation provided the context for Virginia's internal conflicts. By the late 1820s, most other states in the United States had outlawed colonial and early national-era property requirements for voting. A number of states, especially western ones, had also passed laws giving all free white men the right to vote regardless of whether they paid taxes. Not so in Virginia, where only property owners could vote, leaving vast numbers of white men disenfranchised.[11] White male Virginians who could not vote bristled at the inequality. They quite reasonably felt that they had been denied their full measure of liberty, denied their share of the Revolution's heritage.[12] In Fauquier County, white men had another reason to be angry: they suffered under a disproportionate representative scheme that also dated from the colonial era. Under its terms, each county sent two delegates to Virginia's House of Delegates regardless of how many people lived in the county. Because Fauquier was among the most populous in the state, its residents were underrepresented in the legislature. Increasing Fauquier citizens' underrepresentation, and their resentment, the state's senate districts had been drawn to give eastern Virginians proportionately more senators than western Virginians. Addressing the issues of franchise requirements and representation required amending the 1776 state constitution, but that document had not specified an amendment process. Only a new constitution could solve the problem. After decades of protest, western Virginians finally won the battle to hold a new constitutional convention, which met in late 1829 and early 1830.

The Virginia Constitutional Convention gathered some of the most illustrious members of the commonwealth. A very old James Madison, a major author of the U.S. Constitution and fourth president of the United States, was there. Also attending were Madison's successor to the presidency, James Monroe, who had toasted Lafayette and whose estate lay only twenty-six miles from Warrenton; and Chief Justice John Marshall, also part of the Lafayette celebration. Samuel Johnson knew personally some of the other members of the convention: Philip Pendleton Barbour, who had signed a testimonial accompanying Johnson's 1826 petition and who was elected president of the convention; his cousin John Strode Barbour, the U.S. congressman who had also endorsed Johnson's 1826 petition; and John Scott, the Fauquier County attorney and state senator who had played a key role in making sure Johnson's 1811 petition resulted in a law that granted him permission to remain in Virginia.[13]

Because Johnson knew several of the key players and because the discussions of the convention held such relevance for his family, he surely paid attention to what was happening. We can imagine that he turned his ear toward the tavern patrons' conversations about the convention. Newspapers printed many of the speeches, and often men read such things aloud. They wanted the less literate among them to hear and participate in the political discussion, and they also understood that speeches were best comprehended when read as speeches. Samuel Johnson was an unintended beneficiary of this traditional American practice.[14]

When he heard that former president Monroe had emphasized that the Revolution arose from "the doctrine of equal rights," Johnson must have nodded inwardly. Monroe called slavery an "evil" that was "repugnant to . . . State Constitutions and Bills of Rights," and he indicated that Virginia and the nation would be better off without it.[15] Johnson's ears likely also perked up at one politician's suggestion that if Virginia eliminated property requirements for voting, there would be little reason to keep women and free blacks from the polls.[16] (The politician had meant this as an argument for why property requirements ought to remain in place.) Samuel Johnson might have nodded to himself, thinking that he as much as any white man of similar standing deserved to be part of the polity: he *did* own property, and would probably have been able to vote (like his white father) if he were not a man of color.[17]

If discussions about voting rights made Johnson itch to be treated as an equal to whites, the very mention by Monroe of the notion that slaves should eventually be free in accord with the ideals of the Revolution may have helped spark unrest by Virginia's slaves. About that time, reports came to the governor of an unusual number of rumors about slave conspiracies. The governor worried that the rumors "have probably increased the spirit of insubordination" among Virginia's slaves. Especially in an era in which slaveholders were moving to assert their dominance and to protect slavery more aggressively than they had previously, talk of freedom for Virginia's slaves seemed like a match to dry tinder. In order to dampen the insurrectionary spirit among slaves, "militia companies and volunteer organizations went on the alert in fifty-nine Virginia counties as well as in Richmond, Petersburg, Norfolk, and Lynchburg."[18]

The high level of tension among all Virginians—white, black, free, and slave—in late 1829 and 1830 did not compare to the alarm and frenzy that overtook Virginians the following year, when rebellion actually did occur. It is impossible to know the extent to which Nat Turner acted in response to the discussions of 1829–30 and the growing national debate over slavery, but it is clear that his actions fueled both discussion and division on the slavery question—in Samuel Johnson's household as well as in the state of Virginia as a whole.

The gruesome details of Turner's Rebellion, its deeply violent character, engendered strong reactions. The revolt began in the early morning hours of Monday, August 22, 1831, when Nat Turner and six trusted lieutenants traveled toward the Travis farm, where Turner lived and worked. Two more slaves joined them there, and "[a]rmed with axes" the group crept toward the house. Turner snuck in through an upstairs window and came down to unlatch the door and let the group into the building. Once inside, the rebels hacked Nat Turner's masters to death—four people, including twelve-year-old Putnam Moore, who was Turner's actual owner. After leaving to continue their bloody work on another farm, someone remembered that there was a sleeping baby still in the house. Two of them returned to kill the infant. The group proceeded, attacking other families in a similar way, quietly with hatchets and axes rather than shotguns so as not to wake up neighbors. Mostly, Nat Turner served as leader and let others do the killing. From each farm they took necessary supplies, such as horses to aid their movement, firearms for the inevitable conflict with the militia, and brandy to keep themselves going. They also gathered additional recruits at several of the farms, and by morning, there were fifteen rebels, nine on horses. They killed all the whites they could get close to, without regard for sex or age. Sometimes they divided themselves up into infantry (on foot) and cavalry (on horseback), with General Nat calling the orders. By a few hours after sun-up, they had visited seven farms and killed about twenty people. The rebellion seemed to be proceeding just as Nat Turner wanted. But then some slaves betrayed the cause. They began to warn their white masters of the danger. When Turner and some of his followers arrived at the Porters' farm, for instance, they found that the white family had already fled, forewarned by their slaves of the rebellion.[19]

Though Nat Turner's vision of ushering in a new age of black over white was beginning to fade, he led the insurgents forward and the slaughter continued: one child was decapitated as he went to greet two slaves he thought to be friendly, another was killed after his scream revealed his whereabouts, ten more were decapitated at a single farmhouse to which they had fled for protection from their school. Some slaves joined the insurrection voluntarily; others were pressed into service; and before 10:00 a.m. there were forty rebels, all now on horses, ready to kill all the white people. Soon, two separate groups of white men gathered to try to capture the rebels. There now seemed little point in trying to stay quiet, and Nat Turner's army began to use some of the guns they had taken. They marched toward the county seat, Jerusalem, intending to capture the town and take munitions stored there, but soon met up with some of the mounted, armed white men. A battle between the two groups ensued, and during the chaos Turner and a number of his followers managed to escape.[20]

As Turner rested overnight in the woods with some of his men, the alarm spread over Virginia. By the next day, the governor had gotten word and sent forces from Richmond, which was ablaze with fear. Reports came that hundreds of slaves were murdering everyone in their path, an exaggeration of the sixty or seventy men Turner had at the maximum. The news spread to North Carolina, whose governor also sent men toward Southampton County. The several thousand white men raised to battle the insurgents completely overwhelmed Nat Turner's little army, now down to about twenty people hiding in the woods. Turner's group tried to continue the struggle but now encountered resistance everywhere. The rebellion fell apart, its participants either captured or killed, except for Nat Turner, who managed to escape and remain hidden. As white Virginians tallied up the deaths, they found that about sixty white people had been murdered.[21]

White Virginians and North Carolinians exacted their revenge, prowling the forests of the Virginia–North Carolina border for escaped rebels, finding and killing many, but also murdering a number of innocent African Americans. Some white people "joined in the carnage out of sheer racial hatred, having come to Southampton, as one man said, to 'kill somebody else's niggers' without being held accountable for it." But where slaveholders were involved, they tended to restrain themselves; they valued their own property and respected that of fellow slaveholders. They brought many of the suspected rebels to trial. While many rebels met their deaths at the hands of the court in Southampton County, with public funds compensating the owners for their loss, most of those tried there did not. Out of the forty-four slaves and five free blacks they examined, the Southampton justices sentenced sixteen slaves and one free black person to be hanged, and expelled thirteen others beyond Virginia. Those numbers did not include Nat Turner, who remained hidden for over two months. After his capture at the end of October, he explained his actions in his famous *Confessions*, recorded by one of the attorneys at his trial. Inevitably, he was found guilty and hanged, and then Virginians could say that Turner's Rebellion had finally ended.[22]

White Virginians were in shock. There had been other slave conspiracies, but the major ones, Gabriel's Rebellion of 1800 in Richmond and Denmark Vesey's 1822 plan to take over Charleston, had been discovered before they took place. Slave rebellions that had actually occurred tended to be small in vision — a few slaves who became fed up and attacked their masters. Even the massive rebellion in the plantations outside of New Orleans in 1811 resulted in many fewer white deaths than did Turner's Rebellion and was not well known beyond Louisiana.[23] Compared to other slave revolts, Nat Turner's Rebellion, driven by a Revolutionary goal, stood out as extraordinarily successful, bold, and bloody.

After Turner's Rebellion, Virginians saw things differently than they had before. Some white Virginians thought that they ought to rid themselves of such a dangerous population — slaves. For many other white Virginians, viewing the world through the lens of Turner's Rebellion made clear a different truth: free blacks, like the Johnson-Malvin family, had to be removed so that whites might better control their slaves. Free blacks became the scapegoats onto which white Virginians cast their fears.

That was the case in Fauquier County, and Samuel Johnson could not have missed it. Judging from the citizens' petitions they sent to the legislature after Turner's Rebellion, Fauquier County public (white) opinion ran a narrow range from supporting the forcible expulsion of free blacks from the state to endorsing the voluntary and federally funded colonization of free blacks back to Africa. Personally hurtful and perhaps even threatening, thirty-five of the same people who had supported Samuel Johnson's petitions to the legislature now declared their wish to see free blacks leave. Twenty-six of those thirty-five men supported voluntary colonization. They wanted it so badly that they were willing to forgo the states' rights position so clearly articulated by Virginians during the Missouri Crisis and to ask for federal help. They signed printed petitions asking their state legislators to "procure an amendment to the Constitution of the United States, which will give the Congress of the Union, power to pass the necessary Laws" to pay for the passage of free blacks "to the coast of Africa." This scheme's proponents, who included people from four other counties beyond Fauquier, clearly hoped that the plan they endorsed would leave Virginia with a diminishing number of black people, and that those remaining would be properly enslaved. Their ideas mirrored those of many members of the American Colonization Society, which in 1821 began settling an African colony, Liberia, with free and recently freed African Americans.[24]

Among those supporting federal funding for the removal of free blacks, presumably to Liberia, was Samuel Johnson's neighbor John A. W. Smith, who had shown support for Johnson and signed his 1822, 1823, 1824, and 1826 petitions. Also signing the colonization petition were Enoch Foley, who allowed his slave Fanny to buy herself for forty pounds in 1800; John L. Fant, a Warrenton coach maker who later did work on Johnson's house; and Thomas L. Moore, who had helped Johnson become free and who often served as counsel for slaves accused of crimes.[25] Once more, a gap opened up between how whites saw free blacks in general and how they treated those they knew as neighbors, such as Samuel Johnson and his family. The number of Johnson's supporters who now supported the colonization of free blacks also reflected a general shift in white people's attitudes, an increasingly negative view of free blacks that time would strengthen, not reverse.

The many people who signed a petition calling for the outright expulsion of free people of color foreshadowed the more hate-filled future. They included eight of Samuel Johnson's erstwhile supporters, along with one future supporter and over a hundred other Fauquier County men (on all the post-Turner Fauquier County petitions, the signatories were exclusively men). Their petition outlined the logic of expelling free blacks in order to strengthen the slave system: "The undersigned petitioners having long witness[ed] the corruption of the slaves by the free negroes of this commonwealth feel thoroughly convinced that the interest and perhaps the safety and peace of slaveholders if not of the whole white population and the welfare of the slaves themselves, call loudly for the passage of a law excluding free persons of colour from the state." By 1834, the petitioners suggested, all free blacks should be forced to leave except those who "may by a special act of assembly have been permitted to remain," such as Samuel Johnson. If they did not go, the remaining free blacks would be "subject to public sale for the benefit of the literary fund of our state." The petitioners recognized that selling free people into slavery might be "unconstitutional or unwise," and if so, at least all free blacks should have to post bond guaranteeing their good behavior, particularly "not keeping a disorderly house, deal[ing] with slaves nor allow[ing] an unlawful assemblage." If they failed to meet this standard, *then* they might be sold.[26]

The evidence from Turner's Rebellion did not suggest that the presence of free blacks had played any pivotal role. The rebellion had been planned in the woods, not in any free black person's "disorderly house" (unlicensed tavern) nor at any "unlawful assemblage" held at a free black person's home. Slaves, not free blacks, had led the rebellion, and only a couple of free blacks had joined them in carrying it out. But the desire to rid Virginia of free people of color was an old one, as Samuel Johnson personally knew.

In the tavern, eavesdropping on patrons' conversations as he brought food and drink or cleaned up, Johnson must have been disturbed by what he heard in the darkening days of December 1831. This talk of sending free blacks to Africa, a land much farther away and much more foreign than neighboring free states, or of selling free people into slavery did not bode well for his family's future.

But unexpectedly, soon after the new year, came news of other talk—of abolition. A number of the petitions (none from Fauquier) the legislature received after Turner's Rebellion asked that slavery in Virginia be ended gradually and that free blacks be removed.[27] People who wanted to end slavery in the state advocated abolition out of fear, not out of love for liberty or respect for the rights of black people. As a petition signed by over two hundred "ladies" from Augusta County explained, they worried about the "dangers which await us" if Virginia did not rid itself of slavery, a "bloody monster which threatens us."[28] This petition, along with eight others that argued in a similar vein, helped to open a wide-ranging legislative debate on slavery.

What stories Johnson must have had to tell Patty, Lucy, and Spencer when he came home from work in the early weeks of 1832. The tavern was abuzz with the news of what would come to be known as the Virginia Slavery Debate. To the surprise of many, the Richmond *Enquirer*, which had avoided printing articles on a topic it felt to be so delicate, had on January 7 advocated some plan of reducing the number of black people in the state. "Something must be done," the paper declared, about the "dark population [that] is growing upon us." A few days later, under the headline, "Abolition of Slavery," the *Enquirer* printed the news of the beginning of the debate. Thomas Jefferson Randolph, the grandson of the author of the Declaration of Independence, proposed that the voters of the state consider an abolition scheme that Randolph had modeled on his grandfather's plan (never submitted) of the 1770s. The idea was that "the children of all female slaves who may be born in this state on or after the fourth day of July, 1840, shall become the property of the commonwealth." They would then be hired out until enough money had been raised to pay for their deportation beyond the United States.[29]

Some of the men at the tavern must have cursed the suggestion that Virginia voters should consider a gradual emancipation scheme, even if that scheme involved deporting all freed slaves. Johnson's reaction is harder to imagine. Certainly he would have supported abolition. But since Randolph's scheme coupled emancipation with forced colonization, the threat it posed to his family was bigger than the hope it offered to others.

Still, how wonderful it was to hear that some of the delegates spoke grandiloquently in support of abolition and against slavery. Many of those speeches appeared in the newspaper only after the debate had concluded in favor of the slaveholders, but the points they made were not moot. The speeches' publication both in the newspaper and later in pamphlet form showed how much

Virginians were interested in knowing what opponents of slavery had to say.[30] John Chandler had declared that "liberty, rightfully, cannot be converted into slavery." Samuel Moore also spoke of liberty, saying that the maxim that "'all men are by nature free and equal' is a truth held sacred by every American and by every Republican." George Summers went further, claiming that since all human beings had a universal right to liberty, slave rebellions could be justified by that right; a slave could "assert and regain his liberty, if he can."[31]

Predictably, such assertions met stiff resistance from slaveholders, especially those hailing from the state's eastern region where plantation agriculture had begun two centuries before. Alexander Knox said that slavery benefited Virginia's whites because slavery made possible the "high and elevated character which she [Virginia] has heretofore sustained" and was "indispensably requisite in order to preserve the forms of a Republican Government." Others claimed slaves were happy, and that slavery was the best condition for Africans.[32] Samuel Johnson and his family knew that was not true.

If Johnson and his family were trying to figure out how local leaders thought, they found only partial reassurance in the words of Fauquier representative Thomas Marshall, a subscriber to Johnson's 1822 and 1823 petitions. When Marshall weighed in on the slavery debate, he struck a middling position. Marshall did not think slavery was good. He opposed it as a "*practical* evil, particularly in that part of the country with which he was best acquainted — exclusively a grain-growing region; and if all concurred with him, the day would ultimately come, when the evil would disappear." He also possessed a certain tolerance for free blacks, as his support of Johnson's petitions suggested. He said, "[T]here is no evidence of a disposition on their part to join in revolt, or disturb the public tranquillity. They are content to enjoy the limited freedom which the laws permit." Perhaps thinking of Samuel Johnson in particular, Marshall added, "They cling with fond tenacity to the country of their birth." Still, Marshall worried that if the free black population grew too large, free blacks, "having much of the degradation without the salutary restraints of slavery," would eventually "become extremely dangerous." He also opposed abolition and thought the whole subject never should have been discussed. That left Marshall wanting what a number of Fauquier County petitioners wanted: a constitutional amendment that would allow the federal government to support voluntary colonization.[33]

A few weeks later, Thomas Marshall spoke again, this time regarding a bill that would have forcibly removed all "free persons of colour from this Commonwealth." He called the measure "harsh and inhuman" and pointed out that local authorities already had the power to remove free black people who remained illegally in Virginia. It was in the context of this argument that he noted that the existing law was often not enforced because it ran counter to the feelings of most white Virginians. Johnson would have been relieved to hear it, and must have sighed even more deeply when the delegates voted against the forced removal of free black people.[34]

Whatever he thought or felt in the tumultuous winter of 1831–32, it was Samuel Johnson's character to keep it to himself, to listen quietly, and to continue behaving as he had behaved his whole life — "loyal Diligent sober accommodating faithful and honest."[35] Most likely, he saw Turner's Rebellion and the events that followed as reason to be even more accommodating, more deferential than ever before. Now would not be the time to send another petition to the legislature. Now was the time to lie low.

Spencer Malvin held a different view of Turner's Rebellion and its meaning. He carried a strong memory of the worst of slavery, the murder of young Charles. Unlike Samuel Johnson, his sympathies lay clearly with his fellow Afro-Virginians and not with white people. We can imagine that Malvin now saw his father-in-law, who had worked so hard his whole life to gain white approval, as a weak man who bowed to the powers above him and had been afraid even to free his own daughter. Only as her marriage approached had he done so, and now he did not openly assert her liberty. Lucy, loyal to her father, had been blinded into a similar kind of submission, never daring to register as a free black person. Lucy and Samuel were content to stay in Virginia, where their kind was despised, and they did not contemplate leaving even after Turner's uprising. How despicably weak, how lacking in honor, that must have seemed to Malvin.

Spencer Malvin's vision now included freedom for all black people. One did not have to sit by and let things continue, as his father-in-law had so passively done. With the Virginia Slavery Debate, Malvin became aware that even in Virginia some white people wished to see slavery's demise, although he would not have supported the deportation of freed slaves beyond the United States.[36]

Malvin knew that he was not alone in his views. Although the abolitionist movement was not widespread in 1831 and 1832, it was intense. A small group of reformers and visionaries had stepped up the publication of newspapers and pamphlets against slavery. Among them was David Walker, a free black man formerly from North Carolina, whose *Appeal . . . to the Coloured Citizens of the World . . . , and Very Expressly, to Those of the United States of America* constituted an angry cry for immediate action against slavery. Walker called for the widespread mobilization of America's black population. White radicals, such as William Lloyd Garrison, joined the fight as well. Garrison had started his newspaper, the *Liberator*, in January 1831. Later that year he declared boldly that Turner's Rebellion proved him right: slaves wanted freedom, and only "immediate emancipation" could "save [America] from the Vengeance of heaven."[37]

Spencer Malvin came across some of this northern abolitionist literature, perhaps including Walker's *Appeal*, in the months after Nat Turner's insurrection. It stirred his growing radicalism, and he soon began "circulating antislavery papers" and speaking of how the blacks should organize against the whites. He was becoming agitated, and he tried to stir others up as well. Such talk was exceedingly dangerous, especially at a time when white Virginians were so nervous about the black people among them. A new law specified that any slave or free black person who distributed writing "advising persons of colour . . . to commit insurrection or rebellion" would be punished with thirty-nine lashes for the first offense and with death for a subsequent offense. But in the atmosphere of early 1832 such activity was more likely to be punished by a lynch mob before it ever got to court.[38]

Lucy must have begged him to stop. Johnson probably also advised him to be more cautious. Malvin was a man with responsibilities. He had a family to care for. It was his duty to put that concern first, as Samuel Johnson himself had done. Malvin ought not risk his own or his family's safety.

To Spencer Malvin, his father-in-law's argument did not weigh as heavily as the burden of being free and black in increasingly unfriendly Virginia. Malvin and the rest of the family surely heard the news that the only law passed as a result of the great discussion over the future of black people in Virginia was a statute further restricting free blacks and slaves. (The bill supporting state-funded colonization of free black people failed in the senate.)[39]

Even before Nat Turner's Rebellion, Virginia's lawmakers had turned their focus to free blacks, passing in April 1831 a law clarifying the means by which illegal free black residents would be identified and sold. They also reenacted a provision making it a crime to run a school to teach free blacks to read or write. Now they went further. Even though he was *born free*, Spencer Malvin would, under the March 1832 statute, be both tried and punished in the same manner as slaves for any felony or for simple larceny. That is, free black people lost their right to a jury trial in 1832. Except for homicide and other capital cases, they would from now on be brought before a court of oyer and terminer, where only judges heard evidence and gave verdicts. In addition, Malvin, his father-in-law, and all other free black people in Virginia were now barred outright from owning firearms. The provision emasculated black men, who could not protect themselves and their families as white men could. Neither could they preach the gospel if the spirit moved them to do so. Fearing another Nat Turner, the lawmakers had banned all black people, slave or free, from preaching even if the preacher had been licensed and ordained as a minister. Of special relevance to a mixed family of free people, slaves, and former slaves, the law also made it illegal for free people of color to purchase slaves except for their immediate family members. If either Spencer Malvin or Samuel Johnson were inclined to help an enslaved cousin or aunt by purchasing her, he could no longer do so.[40]

Malvin thus had plenty of reason to conclude that Virginia was hostile territory and that he had to leave. And soon, he got word that he was a wanted man. He had better leave fast, but Lucy did not want to go. Fauquier was her home. Moreover, 1832 was the year she gave birth to twins, Rebecca and Thomas Thornton Withers Malvin.[41] She simply could not envision picking up and leaving. And how could she abandon her father and mother? She not only felt a duty to help them, she relied on their assistance to raise her children. She was used to the difficulties of being a "free negro" in an increasingly restrictive Virginia, and she feared being alone in a new place where life might be more difficult than in Fauquier County. It was the same choice her father had faced years before, and she decided as he had. She was not interested in moving north. She would stay in her home.[42]

Not Spencer. One day in 1832, without warning, Spencer Malvin left Lucy, his family, his friends, and all of Virginia behind. His departure demonstrated what Nat Turner's Rebellion had meant to him, and it began a new chapter in the Johnson-Malvin family's lives.

race, identity, and community

SPENCER MALVIN HAD DECIDED who he wanted to be: a free man in a free state where he could freely denounce slavery. His departure forced others to make choices about their identities too. One enslaved man named Sandy chose as Malvin did and fled with him to Pennsylvania; Spencer had not left quite all of his friends behind when he left Virginia. Sandy's owner, John L. Fant (who had signed the petition supporting federal aid to colonize free people of color), explained that in his "decided opinion . . . Spencer Malvin the Husband of Lucy . . . was instrumental in persuading my servant man Sandy to leave the state of Virginia ago to Pensilvania with aview [*sic*] to obtain his freedom."[1] For Malvin, taking an enslaved man with him entailed great risk. Even on his own, Malvin would have been a suspect person — an unfamiliar man of color traveling from a slave state toward a free one. With Sandy, they would cause even more suspicion among Virginia's slave patrols, who had the power to stop and question any black people they saw. In addition the two of them had to worry that once Fant realized that Sandy was gone, Fant might send out designated slave catchers to find his escaped slave, directing them not to stop at the Virginia border but to continue to Maryland and Pennsylvania. Heightening the risk was the fact that by traveling in Sandy's company, Malvin had turned himself into a criminal, as it was illegal to help a slave run off.[2] Malvin made the eighty-odd miles from Warrenton to the Pennsylvania line into much more dangerous territory for himself by choosing to travel with an escaped slave.[3] That he did so points to the strength of his feelings against slavery and his sense of alliance with his enslaved brethren.

An identification with slaves was precisely what Samuel Johnson, and Lucy following him, had sought repeatedly to reject. So when Spencer Malvin "abscond[ed]" from Virginia accompanied by a runaway slave, Lucy and Samuel Johnson did all they could to distance themselves from him and his actions and to reconfirm the Johnsons' relatively privileged place in the community.[4] That took some work because a woman was considered to be one with her husband, and in the wake of Spencer's departure, Lucy would naturally come under suspicion of harboring feelings similar to Spencer's. Lucy's color, which was not associated with social respectability, made the task all the more difficult.

Lucy's and Samuel's efforts to recreate Lucy's identity after Spencer's departure show that they understood that identity was mutable. They worked in the context of community because one forged one's identity within a community and not as an individual apart. And they acted with the awareness that Lucy and her children did not actually have a legal right to stay in Virginia. Recreating Lucy's place in Warrenton would therefore require a multipronged strategy.

The family's actions, and the community's response to them, add more details to our understanding of race in Virginia and of how race as a set of practices changed over time. Turner's Rebellion had made things worse for free blacks, especially in the law, but the on-the-ground reality continued to defy a simple narrative. The Johnson family's insistence on staying put—their small way of making history by asserting their right to stay in the land of their birth—made it necessary that they and their white neighbors find a way to live with one another. And so they did.

Spencer helped Lucy in her quest to divorce herself from his reputation and recreate her life without him by cutting all ties with her. He sent no word of where he was, no note of explanation or apology, and no assurance that he was all right. Perhaps he understood that his silence was necessary if Lucy were to reattach herself to her father's favorable reputation. If so, his silence was an act of love. But more likely, he was simply angry and disgusted with those, like Lucy and Samuel, who did not fight back.

Samuel Johnson seems also to have been angry and a bit disgusted, so he took Malvin to court. Spencer Malvin was long gone, but suing him for debts owed would allow Johnson to exorcise his anger, recover materially from Spencer's departure, and announce to Fauquier's community that he, and implicitly his daughter, disapproved of Spencer's actions. In the summer of 1833 Samuel Johnson went to Thomas Ingram, a justice of the peace, and "complained . . . that Spencer Malvin is indebted to him in the sum of sixty dollars due by account and that the said Spencer Malvin abscond[ed] so that the ordinary process of law cannot be served upon him." In two places on the document that Ingram drew up, the amount Spencer owed Johnson had originally been written as "one hundred & sixty dollars with interest," but had been crossed out and replaced by "sixty." The change betrayed confusion, either on Johnson's part, because he was not quite certain what the amount had been and as an illiterate man kept no records that he could consult, or because Ingram misheard him when he first spoke.[5]

In any case, Ingram believed Johnson's story and ordered the sheriff to bring to court goods of Malvin's worth sixty dollars. The sheriff executed the warrant, conveying to the court Malvin's box of carpenter's tools and a horse cart. Why Spencer Malvin left his valuable tools behind is somewhat perplexing. But they were heavy, and he seems to have wanted to move fast. The existence of a horse cart suggested a horse, which Malvin had apparently used to speed his journey northward. When Spencer Malvin, by then in Philadelphia, failed to appear at the court session a few weeks later, the judges ruled against him for fifty dollars and costs, and they ordered that his goods be sold so that Johnson could recover the debt owed him.

Why did the court rule in favor of Johnson for fifty dollars when he had sued for sixty? Perhaps the carpenter's tools and horse cart constituted the only estate Malvin had left behind, and only amounted to fifty dollars' worth of goods. More likely, the judges were trying to strike some sort of compromise. No record of the loan appears in the court documents, and it is likely that none existed. Johnson was a man of honor with a good reputation, but he also seemed unsure of how much, precisely, Malvin owed him. Fifty dollars was a nice even amount, and by granting that sum to Johnson, the judges could feel that justice, more or less, was done.[6]

The rather spare record of the court case conceals much. It mentions neither that Spencer Malvin was Johnson's son-in-law nor that Malvin had been living in Johnson's house. It gives no sense of when it was that Malvin "abscond[ed]" or when Johnson made the original loan. It demonstrates nothing of the emotional drama that sparked it. But a small detail reveals once again how important it was to white Virginians to draw lines according to race. While Malvin's name appeared on the document without comment, Johnson was referred to in the complaint as "Samuel Johnson (man of colour)." To justice of the peace Thomas Ingram, Johnson's color was of only parenthetical importance, but it was still worth including even though it had no material effect on the case.

Samuel Johnson knew the importance of his status as a man of color, even though he wished it not to matter and wanted to be treated as a full and equal man. He also worried more about Lucy and her children after her husband left. His awareness of color and his concern for Lucy, along with his advancing age, prompted him once again to petition the legislature to allow her to remain legally in Virginia. But what could he say now, after all those previous petitions had failed and after Virginia had turned increasingly hostile to black liberty? That he wanted such permission so that he could free her? No, he had already freed her. That she had performed meritorious service and deserved permission to stay? No, she had not done that. It was Samuel who had earned the affection and support of white Warrenton residents, but that was a generation ago, when the Revolution still seemed recent and well before the cataclysm of Nat Turner's Rebellion. If he petitioned the legislature, would that in itself reveal Lucy's illegal status? Probably, but the petition could be written to obfuscate her tenuous position.

Faced with these problems, Johnson took for his ninth petition a new tack. Realizing that it was he, not Lucy, who was asking for favor, and that as an old man who had been favored before it was he who would be more likely to receive it, Johnson explained—once again through a scribe who drafted the actual document—"that he is getting old and feeble and looks forward in a short time to becoming helpless and dependant." The petition continued, "[H]e has an only daughter, affectionate and industrious, upon whose exertions he may be forced in a short time to Rely for daily sustenance." In other words, Johnson asked that his daughter be allowed to remain in Virginia so that she might care for him, an elderly, "feeble" man of color.[7]

Unfortunately, that was not a particularly convincing argument to the white lawmakers, but the petition made an even less persuasive argument when it explained how duplicitous and untrustworthy black people could be. After its two introductory sentences explaining that Samuel might need to rely on Lucy for help, the petition included this statement:

He would further state that his daughter some years since married Spencer Malvin at that time apparently of unimpeachable character, a thriving intelligent mechanic: but who since has deserted her and his little children. This too under circumstances that go far to shew utter depravity of heart and morals. This desertion was caused by the probable detection of Malvins misconduct in circulating Anti Slavery papers, and in his disclosing a disposition to array the Blacks against the Whites with a view to the supremacy of the former. Your petitioner would call the attention of your Hon bodies to the certificate of Mr Fant concerning the seduction of his negro man from his service by the said Malvin.

John L. Fant's certificate emphasized that it had been Malvin's fault that the slave Sandy had run away. William Phillips, who had signed three other Johnson petitions, added that "said Malvin's persuasions were what induced Sandy to run away & go to Pennsylvania."[8]

How was any of that supposed to help Lucy's cause? Malvin's desertion did not help to explain why Lucy should be allowed to remain in Virginia so that she could care for her father; it showed instead that Lucy needed her father's help and thus counteracted the logic of Johnson's request. And who among the white legislators would want to grant a favor to a young and fertile free black woman whose husband had proved through his antislavery activities exactly why white Virginians should rid themselves of the free black population?

The ambivalence about black people that the petition betrays might have reflected in part the extent to which Samuel Johnson had adopted white values, but it also suggests that Johnson played less of a role in drafting this petition than in drafting previous ones. The petition contained the romantic language coming into vogue at the time, in contrast to the more direct prose people used in the late eighteenth century. It spoke in a voice not so much Johnson's as that of the white man who wrote it and apparently fancied himself a literary stylist. The petition pleaded for sympathy by noting that "after a life of incessant toil," Johnson had "succeeded in procuring for himself a small cottage and Garden where he had hoped to close his Eyes in peace attended by his child—his only child. His attachments to the Town, the County and their people is strong and unalienable. *He* could not at his advanced age and with *his* feeling [go] to another soil and another people, and yet without his daughter and *alone* how could he live here." The plea was not even true, since Samuel would not be left alone without Lucy; he still had his wife, Patty, with whom he had shared so much.

This time, 169 white subscribers supported Johnson's ardent entreaty. Just a bit more than three years after Turner's Rebellion, Samuel Johnson was once again able to gain the favor of many white people, including several who had signed the pro-colonization petition of late 1831.[9] The lawmakers had not similarly softened, however, and the florid prose did not do the trick. The petition arrived at the capital on January 19, 1835, was promptly referred to committee, and was rejected less than a month later on Valentine's Day.[10]

The large number of supporters could nevertheless give Samuel, Patty, and Lucy cause for hope. Nearly half of the subscribers had been women, who in the 1830s began taking a more public and formal political role, especially by signing their names to petitions. Often, they petitioned in support of the work of one of their benevolent organizations—including colonization societies in Virginia and antislavery organizations in the North. Suggesting the existence of some kind of women's organization in Warrenton is that the vast majority of women's names appeared consecutively on two lists, one entitled "Ladies' Names," as if the paper had been passed among them as they gathered together to discuss one of their causes. A number of the women's names were in the same hand, written by someone other than themselves, pointing perhaps to women's lower literacy rate, or perhaps to the fact that signing the petition was mostly symbolic. It was more important that their names appear on the petition than that the women themselves pen them.[11]

The white women's names bespoke personal attachments, or at least charitable feelings, between respectable (white) society and Lucy, who belonged to an undesired group. Those attachments gave Lucy more respectability because antebellum Virginians, and Americans of the era more generally, defined people in context. Who you were could be understood only in terms of who you were connected to. Even race was defined locally and in terms of personal connections. For example, citizens from Lancaster County declared that their neighbor James Corsey was "at least three fourths white" and had been accepted in white society there. Although he had not legally wed his white wife because of the law against interracial marriages, the community accepted the family as legitimate, and they felt that his children should inherit his property. In effect, James Corsey was white even though the community knew he had some African ancestry. By contrast, Wythe County's John Rose, who according to some neighbors had a black grandfather, was understood locally to be a "mulatto." When the matter came to court over the question of whether Rose could serve as a witness against a white man, the General Court deferred to local knowledge. The county court, they decided, could best decide a person's race. Such questions had special relevance after 1833, when, realizing that the 1831–32 laws regarding "free negroes" took away many rights, the legislature adopted a resolution allowing local courts to grant "mixed-blood" people who were not "negroes and mulattoes" a certificate that would protect their rights.[12]

For women of both races, attachments proved especially defining. Only rarely did a woman act as a legal *feme sole*, or woman alone, who owned her own property and transacted her own business. Lucy was far from being a *feme sole*, and hardly appeared as an individual person in the petitions written on her behalf. In the

1835 petition, one sheet of paper containing subscribers' signatures referred to her as "Lucy Johnson (daughter of Sam Johnson)," and in both the petition itself and a letter of support by Judge John Scott (the same man who had helped see the 1812 bill for Samuel Johnson's freedom through to passage) she did not even have a name of her own and was referred to only as Johnson's daughter. Scott wrote, "My acquaintance with the daughter of Samuel Johnson does not enable me to say anything for or against her. I have known her by sight from the time she was a child and that is all I do know of her." In only one of all the documents included in this petition does any sense of Lucy as an individual come through. Even there, the words Ann Norris used to describe her are rather formulaic and flat: "I brought up Lucy Johnson as one of my own children in my house; she was brought [up] by me with all the princapels [*sic*] of honour, honesty, industry and virtue; and allways has practiced the same, and her character, I believe, stands as fair as any other female in the county." Those adjectives described an ideal woman of the antebellum era but did not distinguish Lucy as especially noteworthy or meritorious. Unlike the words used by and about Samuel Johnson, the words describing Lucy make it almost impossible to grasp a sense of who she was or what she was like. As a woman, her personality seems to have been confined to private spaces, whereas her father, as a man and in spite of his color, possessed a public presence and a public personality.[13]

Precisely because Samuel Johnson was a man of note, even if a "mulatto," it helped Lucy that she had again become Lucy Johnson. Her married name appeared just once among the papers included in the 1835 petition, and then parenthetically, on a sheet of paper for subscribers to sign their names. The paper referred to her as "Lucy Johnson (or Malvin)." Her identity as a Johnson once more — her attachment to her father — along with the support of so many white women suggested that so long as Lucy and her children remained in Warrenton, they were probably safe.

The letter from Judge Scott suggested the place the Johnson family then held in Warrenton's community. Scott described Johnson as a "valuable member of the community." He said he would be willing to allow Lucy to stay as a favor to "Sam," whom Scott had "long known and always considered . . . most exemplary in his conduct." Scott concluded with the strange comment, "I believe the white negroes (if you will allow the term) which you have at Warrenton, are a great deal worse than the black bond or free."[14]

Did Scott mean that Johnson and his family were "white negroes," somehow different from black "negroes"? That they acted and perhaps looked more like white people than like free black ones? After all, Johnson was a "bright mulatto" who emulated white values and behavior patterns: he saw that his daughter was properly married, he purchased property, he sued in court, and in general he acted as a patriarch.

Or, more likely, did Scott mean that the Johnsons were free black "negroes" who stood above the "white negroes"? That the Johnsons deserved their place in Warrenton because they actually contributed more than poor white folk whose behavior and possibly their appearance—tanned and dirty—made them appear as "negroes"?[15]

In either case, the paradoxical phrase "white negroes" points us again to the difficulties of race and the problems of belonging. If the Johnsons were the "white negroes" to whom Scott referred, it was their respectable behavior and well-earned place in the community that made them so. They were then "a great deal worse than the black bond or free" because their presence, their anomalous existence in a society divided into white and black, laid bare the illogic of Virginia's racial divisions.

If, however, as Scott probably meant it, the Johnsons were black "negroes," whom he found more worthy than "white negroes," the only reason for their outsider status—their need to request permission for Lucy to remain in Virginia—lay in their blackness. Race here worked to estrange people like the Johnsons, who ought to belong, and to include poor white people—"white negroes"—whose behavior did not warrant their inclusion. Any way that Scott meant it, the term "white negroes" denoted an uncomfortable racial inversion.

That the Johnsons worked so hard to remain in a place that gave rise to a concept like "white negroes" made little sense to people like Spencer Malvin. News of Malvin came through third parties but credibly suggested that he had made a new life in Pennsylvania, eventually finding a new wife. He had chosen a path Samuel and Lucy Johnson had been unwilling or unable to take, a path toward greater freedom in a free state. Philadelphia, especially, offered a large community of free black people who had their own churches, their own benevolent associations, and their own community leaders.[16]

From a modern perspective, Spencer Malvin's choice to leave Virginia may be easier to understand than Samuel and Lucy Johnson's choice to stay. For Malvin, as for the author and abolitionist David Walker, leaving a slave state for a free one constituted an act of resistance against injustice. But for Samuel and Lucy Johnson, it might have appeared that to stay was to resist. In staying, they rejected racial exclusion and claimed their right to participate in their community and to live in their home. They challenged the notion that Virginia belonged to white people.

The Johnsons probably also understood that even beyond Virginia in the free states, whites kept black people from participating fully in their communities. In Philadelphia, one of the centers of the Revolutionary-era antislavery movement, it had become customary by the 1810s to exclude black Philadelphians from the city's public Fourth of July celebrations.[17]

The Johnsons further comprehended that even in Virginia, a place of legally prescribed racial restrictions, white people signed petitions supporting black neighbors. While the Johnsons' choice

to stay may have been motivated partly by fear, the terror of starting afresh somewhere new, that fear had roots in their knowledge
of how race in America worked. They would have had good reason to assume that the family was better off in the slave state of
Virginia, where they had connections both deep and broad, than
in a free state where white people would have little reason to pay
them any special attention or offer any help.

Hoping that his local connections would help him gain for
Lucy a legal right to stay in Virginia, Samuel Johnson petitioned
the legislature again in 1837. Realizing the weaknesses of the previous effort, Johnson in his tenth petition broke from the strategies and words of the 1835 petition. But in so doing he turned
Lucy back into a slave.

The 1837 petition stated that Johnson was "the owner of said
Lucy (his daughter) and consequently of her children." It ignored
the fact that he had once liberated her, because acknowledging
that would have required admitting that she had been living illegally in Virginia for over a decade. Once Lucy had been rhe-
torically, although not legally, re-enslaved, Samuel Johnson could
ask to free her, a request different from the one he had made two
years earlier. After noting (again, probably unhelpfully) Spencer's
departure, the petition explained that Johnson was "getting old
and very much desires to liberate his said daughter and her children before his death but cannot do so without . . . the permission
of the Legislature for them to remain in the state." Appealing to
the legislators' sympathies, the petition told them, "if compelled to
leave the state they [Lucy and her children] cannot possibly in a
land of strangers take care of themselves."[18]

There it was again, the problem of being a stranger. Johnson
and his scribe addressed the issue so briefly probably because they
assumed that everyone who read the petition would understand:
you were who you were connected to; your identity was created in
context; to leave, to be alienated and disconnected, was in some
way to lose yourself.

The forty-two subscribers to the petition emphasized a similar point. They described Samuel and Lucy as part of a community. They bore "testimony to the high respectability of . . . Samuel Johnson" and stated that "his daughter Lucy Malvin is a respectable & useful member of this Community." They concluded by saying that "it would be highly gratifying to your subscribers as well as (in their opinion) to this whole community to grant the prayer of your petitioner."[19] But the petition to free Lucy and her three children, Sam, Rebecca, and Thornton W. (whose full name, Thomas Thornton Withers Malvin, apparently proved too cumbersome), died of neglect. The legislators took no further action on it after they referred it to committee.

Did that mean that Lucy was free or enslaved? When in 1837, eleven years after he first emancipated her, Johnson asked again to free her, did that imply that the community considered her to be his slave once again? Did he think of the emancipation as having expired? Or was claiming her as his slave a sleight of hand to gain legal permission for her to remain in the state? Perhaps the last explanation makes the most sense, but Johnson seems to have been genuinely concerned that his earlier act of manumission had been voided by Lucy's continued residence in the state and that she was no longer free, that she existed in a legal limbo that he needed to rectify.

So he freed her again, even without permission from the legislature. On July 18, 1837, he drafted a second deed of emancipation for his daughter, and this time included his grandchildren too. The deed made no mention of his earlier deed and followed the formula by then established for acts of manumission, stating simply that "for and in consideration of the natural love and affection which I bear to my daughter Lucy Malvin and her children Sam, Rebecca, and Thomas T. [Thornton] Withers . . . who are my slaves [I] do hereby emancipate manumit and set free my said daughter Lucy Malvin and her said children."[20] As with all the other crucial legal acts Samuel Johnson effected, he signed it with his mark, an X.

In one way, Samuel Johnson's second act of emancipation for Lucy—this time including her children—could be understood as a legally shrewd move, making sure that her children had a clear title to their liberty by recognizing the tenuous freedom Lucy, and therefore her offspring, had lived in for the previous decade. Nearly as important, in freeing Lucy for a second time Johnson claimed for her a place in the community as a free woman. Emancipating her again made a statement about who Lucy was and where she stood. What Lucy and her parents wanted everyone to know was that they were proper, respectable citizens.

And proper, respectable citizens did their best to follow the law. When the family learned of a new statute that expanded the county courts' powers to grant free blacks permission to remain in the state, they acted on it. The law stated that as long as all the acting county justices of the peace were summoned and a majority of them appeared, and also that an attorney represented the state, the county justices could grant permission to remain to a free black person who was "of good character, sober, peaceful, orderly and industrious." Unlike the previous provision, the new statute did not specify that any particular act of special merit was needed. Only a bit more than five years after Turner's Rebellion and the anti-free-black sentiment that followed, the legislature relaxed the requirements for allowing free black people to remain in the state. Accordingly Lucy, aided by two white men, made a motion to summon the county justices of the peace to the September 1837 court. Although county officials executed the summonses, nothing further seems to have happened. The case got lost in the docket, and Lucy continued to use opaque language to refer to her status.[21]

An even stronger statement of Lucy's aspirations followed the next year. Lucy was still legally married to Spencer Malvin (assuming that she had in fact been free in 1826 and that the marriage was valid), and only by severing her connection with him could she truly demonstrate her propriety. Respectable citizens did not approve of behavior like his. So, shortly after becoming free again, Lucy asked for a divorce from Malvin. Again, it required a petition. Except in cases of "idiocy," "bigamy," or "natural or incurable" impotence, no one at that time in Virginia could obtain a divorce without a special law allowing it. County courts could grant legal separations, but the separated parties could not remarry.[22]

Never mind that if Lucy had not actually been freed by her father in 1826, then she had never been legally married because slaves could not marry. And never mind that if she had been free the whole time, petitioning the legislature for divorce might alert them to her illegal residence in Virginia. Ignore also that petitioning for divorce was uncommon for white people and almost unheard of for free black Virginians. Forget, too, the small chance of success; during the period in which Lucy petitioned, the legislature rejected about 80 percent of the divorce petitions it received. The Johnsons, valuing respectability, forged ahead. They understood, as did some prominent white Virginians, that the very act of petitioning for divorce made an important social statement. Asking for a divorce could, in and of itself, gain the petitioner a local victory and preserve her reputation.[23]

Supported by the signatures of eighty-five subscribers, almost all of them men, Lucy's divorce petition explained that more than a decade earlier, "Lucy Malvin . . . was . . . married with all the observances of law and of the christian church to Spencer Malvin, a free man of colour." (Temporarily, for propriety's sake, she had to become a Malvin once again. And it was temporary, as the scribe of the petition began writing her name as Lucy Johnson before crossing out "Johnso" and writing Malvin instead.) The petition identified Lucy neither by color nor status, an apparently intentional effort to obscure her dubious claims to freedom and residence in Virginia.

But the rhetorical goal of the petition had little to do with Lucy's legal status; it had to do with her social status, and so the petition focused on showing how unsavory Spencer Malvin was, and how much therefore Lucy deserved to be divorced from him. A central piece of evidence for Malvin's poor character lay in his reaction to Nat Turner's Rebellion: "A few months after the disturbances in Southhampton, Spencer became dissatisfied and insisted on removing to a free state. He made preparations to move off, and without apprising your petitioner (who was averse to the measure) he absconded from his residence (having inveigled a slave by the name of Sandy to go with him[)]." Perhaps more to the point, Malvin had abandoned Lucy, having shown "no inclination to claim your petitioner as his wife, or to acknowledge the obligations of a husband or a father." Instead, Lucy had "been informed, & verily believes that he has forsaken her and his children by her, and has taken another wife with whom he has been living for some years."[24]

Pleading for her own Christian womanliness, Lucy's petition emphasized that she "can exhibit the highest testimonials of character [and] she humbly avouches her past life, in which she has ever respected the laws of the land and the ordinances of Gods [sic] holy Church." She wanted only to continue the behavior that would earn her "the kindness and respect of the world."[25] The petition's subscribers, including A. J. Marshall (Alexander Marshall, one of John Marshall's nephews), whose signature matches the handwriting on the petition, certified that she was "a person of excellent moral character" and that her petition contained true facts. They endorsed her quest for respectability, saying that it was "highly proper to encourage the regard to law & religious observances in persons of her class."[26]

"Persons of her class." Again—the reminder of Lucy's outsider status. Black people were not of the same class as white ones but in crucial ways were expected to behave as if they were. Having shut free black people out of society's center and forced them to the margins, white people nevertheless thought it proper for free blacks to emulate the values of white society.

The problems of belonging, identity, and community arose particularly in Virginia's evangelical churches, so it is not surprising that for Lucy they surfaced in the context of her efforts to follow the "law & religious observances" when she sought a legal divorce. In the Revolutionary era, evangelical churches, especially Methodist and Baptist congregations, began trying to convert slaves to Christianity. They had great success, and by the 1820s they even "tolerated black evangelicals' persistent attempts to exercise spiritual leadership," that is, to preach the gospel. White church leaders had by then resolved the question of how slaves could also be fellow church members — or how fellow church members could be enslaved — through paternalism. Religious fellowship, they decided, did not necessitate equality in this world, but it did require that whites guide and "parent" the black people under their care. Turner's Rebellion challenged that sentiment, as "white evangelicals wondered what it meant that the rebel had claimed to be a preacher." After the rebellion, white church members allowed blacks much less autonomy within the church and instead turned their attention to the "mission to the slaves," a concerted drive to better slaves' condition by bringing them the gospel, but not earthly freedom. The proslavery mission's organizational effect was to segregate black people into their own meetings and even their own buildings, but always with white oversight. Lucy was caught up in this dynamic, on the one hand welcomed in fellowship because she essayed to follow the path of a proper Christian woman, and on the other excluded with the words and reality of being one of the "persons of her class."[27]

When the lawmakers, predictably, rejected Lucy's divorce petition just two days after they received it, the Johnson family decided that they were finally done with petitioning. Out of the eleven petitions they had sent, only the first had succeeded, and over time the legislature had become less and less disposed to grant their requests. At least in the early 1820s it seemed only a glitch here or there had prevented Samuel's obtaining permission to free his family members, but now the legislators' message was clear: they would not extend favors to black Virginians. The Johnson family finally heard it.

Still, they did not choose to leave for a place where they could be more securely free. Still, they chose to maintain their local identity in their local community.

The irony is that their local identity on the margins—even if they wished to be in the center—could prove useful, as it had in the years when Samuel Johnson had not paid any taxes. Lucy, who was effectively if not legally single, could do something that would have been much more difficult for a white woman in her position. She could ignore propriety and white social mores when they did not fit. Just like Spencer Malvin, she could remarry even though she was legally still wed (assuming her marriage to Malvin had been valid).

So she did remarry. Her new husband, Sandy Elkins, was a slave (another with a last name), so what did the law have to do with it anyway? Even if she were free, Elkins was not, and their marriage could have no legal standing. Without the formal Christian ceremony or the legal validity of her first marriage, Lucy Johnson Malvin wed Sandy Elkins sometime in the year or two after her failed divorce petition. He was a little over thirty years old at the time, and she was around thirty-five. Perhaps she had already fallen in love with Elkins well before the marriage, which likely took place between 1839 and 1841, and the new romance had helped to convince her that she should request a divorce.

Since Lucy valued respectability, marrying an enslaved man seems an odd choice. But Sandy Elkins resembled Spencer Malvin and Samuel Johnson in important ways that Lucy clearly recognized. Elkins was a "bright mulatto" and a skilled mechanic. Enslaved to a coach maker in the 1840s, his skills went beyond coach making to repairing fences, making iron fixtures, and hanging gates. He knew his birth year (1808) unlike Johnson but like the free-born Malvin. In addition, like both Johnson and Malvin in their different ways, Sandy Elkins yearned for freedom and eventually obtained it.[28]

Sandy Elkins, Lucy's new husband, may have been the same person as the enslaved Sandy who ran away to freedom in Pennsylvania with Spencer Malvin but was "recovered by his master." John L. Fant, the owner of the runaway Sandy, was a coach maker like Sandy Elkins's owner a decade later. And in 1830 Fant owned several slaves who were of an age to have been Sandy Elkins. It is conceivable that after Fant recovered Sandy, he was willing to deal with him as so many owners were willing to deal with slaves who wanted freedom: by making an agreement rather than by punishing him harshly or selling him south. Fant might have promised never to force Sandy to leave Fauquier if Sandy would work faithfully for him; Fant might have allowed Sandy to earn some cash on his own; or maybe he agreed to sell him to a different owner, such as Charles Bragg. If the runaway Sandy was in fact Sandy Elkins, Lucy gave up nearly all of her propriety by marrying him. If indeed they were the same person, and if Lucy had already formed a liaison with him several years before their marriage, we can better understand why even her divorce petition would mention that Malvin had "inveigled" Sandy to go with him. The blame for Sandy's improper behavior could be laid firmly at the absent Malvin's feet, and Sandy might retain some of his own reputation as a good slave and skilled worker.[29]

In a society with social prescriptions as strict as those of antebellum Virginia, propriety could be a heavy burden. It was not only free blacks, but white people too, who found loving someone "improper" to be both risky and sometimes unavoidable. If identity was formed in a web of connections and in the context of community, plenty of people compromised their social identities by loving someone who lived on the other side of one of the many lines—of race, class, freedom, sex—that divided Virginia's society.

Lucy knew one of those people pretty well. She had named her third child after him. Dr. Thomas Thornton Withers also later served as executor of her father's estate. Withers had unusually close connections with black people. He never legally married, but the first item in his will suggests a long-time love. When he wrote the will shortly before the end of the Civil War, he declared, "I free Eliza Pleasants & such of her children and grandchildren as belong to me and direct my Executor to pay to her for her own use one Thousand Dollars and also give to her the brick house on Culpeper Street, with an additional sum sufficient to remove them beyond the State of Virginia. I also free Lucy Jackson and her children with enough money to convey them out of the state."[30] Later in the will, after giving his library and watch to his brother Robert, he specified that Eliza should also receive "one Bed & the Tea & Table China & Cutlery." A small number of white people freed their slaves upon their deaths, and some even provided for the slaves' removal out of the state, but giving a slave such a large sum of money as well as a brick house, a bed, and china was exceedingly unusual. Eliza showed her own affection for Withers, or at least her desire to remember him, by purchasing from his estate a bookcase.[31] Thomas T. Withers was most likely married after all—to his slave Eliza Pleasants, whom he honored by using her full name.

Because Doc Withers was a man and a prominent citizen, the community might simply wink and nod at such behavior. For a white woman of low social status, the rules were different. Paulina Martin and her free black lover, William Hughes, were summoned before the court in 1848 for "commit[ting] fornication together, against the act of assembly." (Perhaps William Hughes was a relative of the Philip Hughes who, a generation before, had also been in a relationship with a white woman.)[32] By the next year, neither Paulina nor William could be found in Fauquier, as "it is said that they have left the County." If either of them had hope of belonging, they would have to do it in a community other than Fauquier County.[33]

Peering into the relationships, tracing some of the webs of connection between Warrenton's residents, leaves us as perplexed as does the term "white negroes." Virginia had lots of rules, many of them inscribed in law, about how people ought to behave and with whom they should associate. As we have seen, white and black Virginians violated them all the time. It turns out to be much easier to make up such rules than to follow them, because human beings recognize one another even across the lines of hatred or hierarchy that they draw. The full arc of Samuel Johnson's life depended on this fact. As much else as had changed in Virginia in the 1820s and 1830s, this human truth had not. The triumph of human connection over socially constructed divisions—free Lucy Johnson Malvin's loving enslaved Sandy Elkins, white Doc Withers's loving black Eliza Pleasants, white Paulina Martin's loving black William Hughes—may be precisely what convinced Samuel Johnson that he belonged in Fauquier County, that unlike Spencer Malvin he would remain in Virginia even though it was a slave state, and that he would die before he left.

CHAPTER SIX

legacies

SAMUEL JOHNSON DID DIE before he left. Or, rather, he left only by dying.

Johnson had long feared what would happen upon his death. If he believed in heaven he could be pretty sure that he would go there, but he feared death with the particular set of worries of a man who owned his family as his slaves. The winter of 1836, when he was about sixty-one years old, must have brought special concern, for that is the year he wrote his will. Even a casual glance at early nineteenth-century wills shows that most people drafted them shortly before they died; they knew death was coming. But in 1836 Samuel Johnson was wrong. The crisis passed, he found himself well, and he redoubled his efforts to take care of earthly business before his eventual passing.

The final years of Samuel Johnson's life form only part of the final chapter of his story, which continued beyond his life. He had intended it that way. He had lived with his eye toward the future, toward providing for his children and grandchildren, toward creating a legacy of freedom. The extent to which he achieved the goals he set for himself early in the nineteenth century can be measured best by following the events that occurred beyond his life. Measuring the meaning of his story is a more subjective endeavor, but that Samuel Johnson's life had meaning, that it mattered that he lived and struggled, cannot be in doubt.

Samuel Johnson lived his final years in something approaching refinement and surrounded by loved ones. Despite all the failed petitions to the legislature, despite the shock and embarrassment of Spencer Malvin's absconding, Johnson could see that he was better off than many white people. His family — Patty, Lucy, and his grandchildren — all lived with him in a comfortable home. Even if the family might have preferred that Lucy's husband were free so that he and Lucy could live in their own household, it must have brought Samuel and Patty comfort and joy to watch their grandchildren grow.[1]

The house in which they lived possessed a certain grace, including items that were not purely necessary but objects of comfort. The most valuable was the feather bed, which with a bolster and pillows made a nice place for Samuel and Patty to sleep. They also owned some substantial pieces of furniture: a sideboard, a cupboard, a table and six chairs, and a walnut chest. The table was old, probably because it had been one of the first items Johnson had bought when he was newly free, but it still provided a center for family life. As they sat together to eat, the family could look at the several framed pictures on the walls. Two mirrors also provided decoration in addition to serving their more functional role. Johnson did not have the high-class objects, like a pocket watch and books, that Doc Withers did, but the family was comfortable.[2]

Providing material security and comfort to his family partially fulfilled his long-time goal to be fully a man, and he wanted to ensure that this provision would continue after he died. A number of legal problems stood in the way, however. First, heirs and descendants had to be free, not enslaved. In case all else failed, he would free them in his will, which in 1836 included emancipation provisions for Patty, Lucy, and the

grandchildren. It was the next year that he decided to emancipate Lucy again during his lifetime and that he drafted his
second deed of manumission after his final, failed plea to the
legislature.[3]

In addition to making sure that his family would be free after
his death, Johnson wanted to know that they would benefit from
all the property he had amassed. One transaction, though, had not
gone quite right. Several years before, Johnson had made a contract to purchase a "small lot of ground lying within the corporate
limits of the town of Warrenton, between the Tavern of William
Wattie and the main street." Johnson had made the agreement
even though at the time he did not have the eighty or so dollars
he and the seller, John Leary, had agreed to. Johnson was used
to such arrangements; it was how he had purchased himself decades before. As with the contract to purchase his own freedom,
other people held the crucial paperwork. This time it was Thomas
Digges, a relative of his former owner Edward Digges. Johnson
understood that an illiterate free black man could be quite vulnerable when it came to legal matters and that involving a trusted
white person was a wise move. But it also disempowered Johnson,
who depended on both Leary and Digges to make sure the transaction was completed.[4]

By the summer of 1837, Johnson was certain that he had paid
Leary the required sum, and was angry that he had not received
title to the land. He had twice before brought legal suits, against
Thaddeus Norris in 1818 and against Spencer Malvin in 1833, and
had both times won. So he followed a familiar path and took
Leary to court. The presiding judge was none other than John
Scott, who had so long ago helped Johnson obtain his freedom.

The original bill of complaint indicated that Johnson did not
quite remember when he and Leary had made the agreement
or exactly how much he had agreed to pay. The complaint read,
"[S]ometime in the year —— he entered into an agreement with
John Leary for the purchase of a small lot of ground . . . for which

your orator was to give the sum of Eighty dollars as well as he recollects." Johnson further explained that the note outlining the purchase "was placed in the hands of Thos. E Digges for safe keeping, and that said Digges now informs him that said memorandum is unfortunately lost or misplaced." Johnson indicated that he had been trying for some time to resolve the manner outside the legal system, "but he now despairs of ever effecting a settlement otherwise than through the merciful interposition of your Honor."

In response, John Leary the next year explained to the court that Johnson was wrong on several counts. Unlike Johnson's complaint, the literate Leary's response included specific details with written evidence to support them: it was April 21, 1830, when they made the agreement; the amount was $97.75, not $80, and Leary had a copy of the bond to prove it; Johnson had paid nearly all of the money due, but still owed over $9 in both principal and interest; and Leary *had* given Johnson a deed to the land. That last part of the story was strange. Leary claimed that he, Johnson, and Thomas E. Digges had gone together to the clerk's office "for the purpose of having said deed recorded." But when they got there, "for some cause not distinctly recollected by this respondent, it was not effected. T. E. Digges having charge of the deed, laid it on one of the desks in the said office, and forgot it." The deed remained lying on the clerk's desk, while Johnson and Leary "retired" from the room. "[S]hortly afterward," Leary walked by the "door of the office, on his way out, saw the paper, and put it in his pocket." Since Johnson did not ask for a copy — "No demand has been made on this respondent for it"— and because "the balance due was not paid," Leary had retained the deed.[5]

After obtaining depositions from key witnesses in the spring and fall of 1838 (court cases dragged on in the nineteenth century just as they do today) and examining the written evidence, Judge Scott decided that Johnson did still owe Leary money.

When Johnson paid it on January 28, 1839, the court made sure that Johnson got a copy of the deed, and nearly nine years after he agreed to buy it and two years after he filed suit, Samuel Johnson finally had his plot of land in town, right near its center.

As with so much else, this small drama showed both Johnson's desire to fit in and his persistent outsider status. What could be more American, and more standard, than investing in real estate? What better demonstrated wanting to be at the center of things than buying land near the center of town? Johnson pursued this desire even at a time of increased racial fears in Warrenton. In the mid-1830s town authorities had appointed watchmen to "suppress all disorderly meetings of coloured persons" by jailing any free or enslaved black people found outside after ten o'clock at night.[6]

Even suing in court showed Johnson's desire to fit in. Suing when a transaction went awry was very common behavior, part of how Virginia men did business. On the surface, Johnson appeared to be just another litigious Virginian, with his race mentioned nowhere in the trial records. But his slave past, his illiteracy, continued to hurt him and to mark him as different. Giving the key paperwork to a third party was unusual, and Thomas Digges, as it turned out, was a bad choice. Not only did Digges carelessly leave the deed on the clerk's desk (if we believe Leary's story), but he lost the original contract, something Johnson would have been unlikely to do. Yet Johnson was forced to turn to Digges or someone like him because as an illiterate person he could not manage his own business.

Lucy, by contrast, could sign her name. Presumably, she could also read at least simple things. But she did not have confidence in her skills; she sometimes signed documents with her mark, and when she did write out her name, she did so tentatively, leaving a slightly shaky (but legible) set of letters. (Readers can view her mark and her signature, as well as her father's mark, online.)[7] Although it was not quite true, as Ann Norris said, that Norris taught Lucy as she taught her own children, at least Lucy had some important skills with which she could help her father negotiate the complicated legal business the Johnsons engaged in.

And the years 1836–38 had been full of business: Samuel wrote a will, sued John Leary for the land Johnson had bought, petitioned for Lucy's freedom, and emancipated her in a deed of manumission. Lucy, for her part, sued for divorce and then remarried despite the failure of the divorce petition. After that flurry of activity, the family settled down again. They had succeeded only in gaining the plot of land in Warrenton. Permission for Lucy to remain in Virginia and a clean divorce from Spencer Malvin remained outside their grasp.

Johnson, true to his personality, continued to hope for the best, but toward the end of his life he did finally make plans for what he had so long fought against: his family's removal beyond Virginia. His 1836 will revealed his thinking on this matter. After emancipating his family and "solemnly renounc[ing] all title to and interest in" them, his will designated three trustees to manage his estate. Johnson asked that the trustees "endeavour to obtain permission for my wife, Daughter and grandchildren . . . to remain in the Commonwealth of Virginia." If that failed, and Johnson had to know that it probably would, he asked that the trustees sell his property to fund the family's move "to such non-slaveholding state" as they chose. Any remaining funds would be turned over to the family, with Patty and Lucy getting equal shares. Making plans, even contingent ones, for his family to leave Virginia was a difficult thing to do, because accepting failure was not in Johnson's nature.[8]

Samuel Johnson in his mature years understood that life for African Americans in Virginia had become more difficult, and he also recognized that his friendships with white people, which he relied upon, were under great strain. That is perhaps why he chose so many trustees, all men from prominent families, to carry out his wishes. He said that he hoped the three would "befriend me in this behalf," but he did not count on it. If one or two of the trustees decided not to "befriend" him, the remaining one(s) might. The final section of Johnson's 1836 will further revealed the doubts he then held about the extent to which white people would help his family: "In case of the death or refusal to act of either of the Trustees hereinnamed [*sic*], I desire that the purposes of this, my last will, may be carried into effect by the survivors or survivor."[9]

Johnson's will stood in contrast to the bulk of his activities at that time. He continued to build—literally—a life for himself and his family. Ten years before, in 1826, he had sold part of his land near the well square, and sometime after that he purchased, in addition to the town lot bought from John Leary, another, larger lot on Winchester Street.[10] Although the evidence is sketchy, it seems that Johnson began to build a house on this lot sometime in the early 1840s, shortly before he died. And he hired John L. Fant, the coach maker and owner of the runaway Sandy, to construct parts of his new house.[11]

Samuel Johnson's planning for his family's future continued almost to the very day he died. In early August 1842 he was feeling weak and realized he needed to add a codicil to his will to make provision for his two new grandchildren, Edinborough and Jasper, who had been born to Lucy and Sandy Elkins in the previous few years.[12] As he had done so many times in his life, Johnson asked a white, educated friend to help him. On August 10, almost exactly thirty years since his rebirth into freedom, Johnson made his last public, legal act. The codicil noted that since he had first written his will, Lucy "has again married and has other children." Johnson wanted those children and any future children to be freed and provided for equally to Sam, Becky, and Thornton Malvin.[13]

Patty had already died, which we know only because another legal document, recorded much later, happened to mention it.[14] As with Sam Jr.'s death, no public or cemetery record of Patty's death remains. She was born and died in obscurity, a legal slave her whole life. (Johnson's emancipation of her would only have taken place if he had died first.) Samuel and Patty were together nearly four decades, an impressively long marriage by any standard. Besides the big things they had shared—the two children they had together; the loss of their son, Sam Jr.; and the emotional ups and downs of their daughter's life—they had shared so many smaller, daily experiences. They had made a home together.

One can imagine that it was Patty's death that weakened Samuel in the summer of 1842. Writing the codicil to his will signaled that he once more felt death growing near, and this time he was right. He died a few days later, in mid-August 1842, and joined Patty again.

Samuel Johnson had held his family together until the end, even if that meant that Patty had remained his slave until her death and that Lucy and her children resided in Virginia illegally. He had been a man of great will and intelligence, an honorable, honest, and likeable person who, through persistent struggle and unflagging determination, had done more for himself and his family than most black men in Virginia were able to do. Although he failed to achieve his ultimate goal of full freedom for his family in Virginia, the fault was not his, but Virginia's. And if he wanted release from the struggles of his life, he finally found it—not by moving away from Virginia to a free state, not by winning special dispensation from the legislature, but only in death, which liberated him from the cares of the world.

That was the limit that Samuel Johnson's experience demarcated: black men in antebellum Virginia could become legally free, but they could not live freely. They could build friendships with white people and they could become important to their communities, but they were barred from claiming a place for themselves as *men*. They could not vote or participate in public life (except for working on the roads), and most important they could not protect and provide for their families as white men could. Samuel Johnson pushed against the limits set by law and society, but in the end he could only nudge them a bit. He could not break them down. His life on the margin, and pushing against the margin, undercut some of white Virginia's assumptions about race and social place, and his story challenges some of our own assumptions about how race worked in antebellum Virginia. But the greater point is that race *worked*. It took repeated effort, but in ways that mattered deeply race did effectively divide white from black—from birth to death.

Despite his efforts, Samuel Johnson's death left Lucy in a precarious position: probably free, definitely not white, partially literate, and legally unempowered. According to the terms of Johnson's will, his property did not go to Lucy directly but to a trust. The trustees, not Lucy, had to manage the business relating to Johnson's estate. Of the three men Samuel Johnson designated as trustees, only Doc Withers was willing to take on the responsibility. But Withers seems to have made no act to gain for Lucy and her children permission to remain in Virginia, and of course her husband was enslaved, so Lucy had little choice but to stay in Warrenton and hope that the county officials never decided to enforce the 1806 law.

If, however, Sandy were free, they would be mobile, and they could find a more hospitable place. With Samuel gone, Lucy and Sandy Elkins could now follow their own destiny. Gaining Sandy's freedom would figure centrally in their plans.

First, Lucy had to settle some financial matters. After her parents' deaths, Lucy had continued to have work done on the new house. Since she and Sandy had little income, she amassed significant debts in the process. The debts could be repaid only by selling some of the family's real estate, but Virginia law was written to protect real estate, especially when held by a trust, as it was in Lucy's case. Only with a court order could the property be sold.

It is hard to know how much this issue weighed on Lucy. She might have wanted to sell some land not only to pay off debts but to help Sandy purchase his freedom. But caring for her seven children kept her exceedingly busy. In addition to Sam, Becky, and Thornton Malvin; and Edinborough and Jasper Elkins; she and Sandy had two more children, Robina and Jerome, whom Samuel Johnson never met. The survival of so many children indicates relatively good health for both Lucy and the little ones — enough good food to eat, a generally healthful environment, and no major epidemics. It was a blessing to have so many children around, but a challenge too.[15]

In the end it was not Lucy but rather her creditors who initiated the legal proceedings that would allow her to sell some land and pay her debts. At the top of the list was John L. Fant, who had done most of the work to build the new house. He took Lucy and her children (the trust was on behalf of all of them) to court in August 1847, asking that a "decree may be made directing a sale of the vacant lot on Jail Street," the one Johnson had sued John Leary for, as well as "a portion of said [larger] lot on Winchester street, such portion as will not affect the value of the remainder." Fant requested that "out of the proceeds of sale" he be paid "the amount [of $392.49] . . . due to him."[16]

Lucy agreed to this plan, as did the trustee Doc Withers, while the attorney appointed to defend the children turned the matter over to the court to decide on the children's behalf. The case moved quickly, and a few months later the designated lot on Jail Street (today's Waterloo Street) and part of the larger lot, including a "comfortable House" and a "Blacksmith shop," were sold at auction. After paying Fant, a second creditor named William H. Gaines, and court costs, Lucy netted $256.27. One of the court papers indicates that the purchaser, John Smith, acted in cooperation with Lucy and her creditors, for he "agree[d] that the House and lot . . . shall be set down to Miss Lucy, Dr. Jones, and John L. Fant as the purchasers." Presumably Lucy would use the cash from the sale to repay Smith, and she would get to keep her house, while Fant and Jones would also forward cash to Smith and would then own some portion of the lot.[17]

The papers of this relatively straightforward court case help-
fully included a number of personal details about Lucy's life
that would otherwise have been lost. It is only because of this
case that one learns that Lucy Johnson Malvin married Sandy
Elkins, as it identified Lucy as Samuel Johnson's "daughter who
is usually called Lucy Elkins (she having married a slave named
Sandy Elkins)." The document also named the four children they
had together, while Samuel Johnson's will had referred only to
Lucy's "other children." In addition, Fant's bill of complaint revealed that Patty died before Samuel, and explained how the designated trustees behaved after Johnson's death. Johnson had had
good cause to fear that even after a lifetime of good citizenship he
might not find white friends willing to act as trustees. It was not
simply that Robert E. Scott and Alexander Marshall, the likely
writer of Lucy's divorce petition, were unable to take on the duties of trustee; they "wholly refused to have anything to do with
the trust."[18]

It is also because of *Fant v. Elkins* that we know that Lucy's
property included a blacksmith's shop, which poses a bit of a puz-
zle because it stood at a time when its occupant, Sandy Elkins,
was still enslaved. Either Lucy and Sandy planned for his freedom and constructed it so that he would have a workspace after
his emancipation, or else his owner allowed him to work there on
his own time. As late as 1850 Sandy probably still lived with his
owner Charles Bragg and not with Lucy and their children. But
maybe the Census entry of 1850, which lists a slave of Sandy's age
in Bragg's household, refers to another person, and Sandy did live
with his family. (Where Lucy was in 1850 remains a mystery; her
name does not appear in that year's Census.)[19] It is even possible
that Sandy had made an arrangement like the one that Frederick
Douglass made with his master in Baltimore in the late 1830s:
young Frederick lived and worked completely independently but
turned over a portion of his earnings to his master. The arrangement between Douglass and his owner so irritated Douglass that

he decided to go somewhere where he could keep all of his earnings, and he escaped from Baltimore to the North in 1838. Sandy, married and firmly attached to his family, could not make that choice. But he did keep his hopes and efforts set on eventual freedom.[20]

Other scraps of valuable information also emerge from *Fant v. Elkins*. We learn that, having once supported her divorce petition to Spencer Malvin, the Warrenton community now viewed Lucy's marriage to Sandy as legitimate even if extralegal. William Gaines, for one, did not hesitate to accept money from Sandy Elkins for debts owed on Samuel Johnson's account. He noted that "on the 30 March 1846, he has received of Sandy Elkins, the husband of Lucy Elkins five dollars." Finally, the papers in *Fant v. Elkins* contain the only evidence of Lucy's literacy: she signed her name when acknowledging receipt of the cash due to her, although she signed only with her mark on the response to Fant's bill of complaint.[21]

The impression left by *Fant v. Elkins*, one of the last Fauquier County records mentioning the Johnson family, is a somewhat sad one. Samuel Johnson, and Lucy following him, did manage to establish their family in the town center and build a substantial house there, but Lucy struggled mightily to make it all work. She and Sandy together simply could not afford to keep up the modest lifestyle Johnson had managed to build. Fant's complaint emphasized the meager resources Lucy had at her disposal, as well as her honest efforts to repay her father's debts. It explained that Johnson "possessed very little personal estate, which has been applied to the payment of funeral expenses and debts and in order to save the real estate, the said Lucy Elkins has from her own earnings paid many debts of the testator."[22]

Things got a bit easier in 1852, when, in keeping with family tradition, Sandy Elkins managed to convince his owner to emancipate him. The deed of manumission included only formulaic language, so we can only guess at the "divers good causes" that motivated Charles Bragg to free his "slave Sandy Elkins a bright mulatto man." Surely, Sandy's desire to lead an independent life—a desire clearly in evidence in the blacksmith's shop that stood on the lot Lucy owned—figured large as one of the "good causes" the deed mentioned. Elkins was "about forty-five years" old when he became free. He had already given the bulk of his working years to others, which likely made it easier for Bragg to consider freeing him. That same year, Sandy did some work "repairing woodwork, making new irons & hanging three gates for the Court house lot." The next year, 1853, he dutifully registered with the Fauquier County clerk as a "free negro." Those are the last records of the family in Fauquier County.[23]

Although Lucy and Sandy Elkins shared with Samuel Johnson a deep desire for full freedom and a wish to keep their family together, they did not share Johnson's commitment to Virginia. By 1860 the Malvin-Elkins family lived in Washington, D.C., where Sandy worked as a blacksmith. Washington was a good choice. Not Virginia, but not far away either, Washington provided both a familiar culture and the assurance of freedom. No longer did the family need to fear re-enslavement or deportation. With its growing population, Washington also offered financial opportunities for a skilled blacksmith who could make gates and fences for new buildings and repair carriage wheels battered by the city streets.[24]

In 1860 the Census taker found Sandy living in Washington with his children and stepdaughter, Rebecca Malvin. Rebecca worked in "service," that is, as a maid, and at age twenty-eight probably also helped to run the household. Her half brother Jasper, then eighteen years old, worked as a blacksmith. Edinborough, twenty, also had a skilled trade; she was a seamstress. The other children, though teenagers (Robina was sixteen and Jerome fifteen) did not attend school, and so presumably worked as well. The family had made measurable progress upward, which would have made Samuel Johnson proud: they had significant property, and unlike Johnson his grandchildren could read and write.[25]

Missing from the household were Lucy and her first two sons, Samuel and Thomas Thornton Withers Malvin. Thornton, also sometimes known as Thomas T. W. Malvin or as "Doc," worked, like his grandfather, as a waiter. He lived with his eighteen-year-old wife and one-and-a-half-year-old baby. The young family could not afford their own apartment and instead boarded in another person's home. Thornton, the Census taker noted, was illiterate; Lucy's literacy skills had not been strong enough to ensure his own, and so he had not done as well as his younger Elkins half siblings. But Thornton had hope of a better life; his wife was skilled, a dressmaker—maybe he met her through his half sister Edinborough—and she was literate and would be able to teach their children.[26]

The fate of Samuel Johnson's namesake Samuel Malvin was recorded in 1860. At the age of thirty-two he had died of consumption, or tuberculosis, which usually killed slowly as its victims seemed to waste away from the inside, losing weight, coughing badly, and spitting up blood. Lucy did not live long enough to mourn this loss. She had died by then.[27]

As was true for her brother and mother before her, Lucy's death went unrecorded. We cannot even be sure that she left Fauquier with Sandy and the children, but we know that she did not get to see all of her children grow up. When she died, she might still have worried about her children's status, afraid that they might someday again be reduced to slavery. She did not know that soon slavery would be illegal everywhere in the United States, for she did not live to see the Civil War, which began in 1861, the Emancipation Proclamation of 1863, or the passage in 1865 of the Thirteenth Amendment outlawing slavery.

Lucy lived and died in an era of slavery and deeply held racism, but she had managed to keep her children with her and her family together. She had kept moving toward freedom and independence. As of 1860 she had, together with Sandy, arrived at those goals. In that way she honorably fulfilled her father's dreams. But as a woman, Lucy was never able to achieve the sort of position in the community that her father had earned. Neither did she or any of her children or grandchildren enjoy the close relationships with powerful people from which Johnson had benefited. For Lucy, that fact reflected her gender, her lower place as a woman. Her children's relative obscurity sprang from a different cause: they grew into adulthood in a time and place without slavery.

Ironically, it was easier in the era of slavery than later for an uneducated free black man to win the support of U.S. congressmen, lawyers, and state leaders. Relatively secure in their dominance, the southern white men and women of the antebellum era could condescend to help a deserving person of African descent. It made them feel just and good, and it helped them fool themselves into thinking their social system was fair and reasonable. They could convince themselves that the mass of black people deserved to be where they were and that when someone like Samuel Johnson rose above that lowly station, white people would recognize and support the effort.[28] In a society with a relatively small and deeply interconnected group of elites, coming to the attention of one state leader led easily to connections with others, as Johnson's experience demonstrates so clearly.

The anomalous population of antebellum free black Virginians might sometimes prove threatening, but not nearly so threatening to whites as the large numbers of free black people living in the era after slavery. Antebellum Virginia was an awful place in which to be black, but for people like Johnson it was better than what followed.

Samuel Johnson and his family's story is thus specific to his time and place, but it speaks to broad themes. Like all history, it consists in both change and persistence. We should not underestimate the significance of the changes Johnson saw during his life, or the changes that Lucy and her children saw afterward. But the persistence of race as something that mattered—the 1860 Census, like those that followed, marked people by race—strikes one more forcefully. Had race not existed, Johnson's life would have been utterly different from what it was.

The story of Samuel Johnson and his family also underscores how much we all are part of history, no matter how obscure or unknown we might be. We all work together in our daily lives to create the worlds in which we live, whether we think about it that way or not. We, like Samuel Johnson, like Spencer Malvin, like Lucy Elkins, make decisions about our lives, our identities, and our relationships in ways that help create our own moment in time. But of course our decisions are constrained, as Johnson's were, by the historical circumstances in which we find ourselves. There was nothing Johnson could do to change the 1806 law, nothing he could do to stop Turner's Rebellion and its aftermath, no way to single-handedly alter Virginia's racial order. History makes us as much as we make history. And it is in that intersection, that dynamic interplay between an individual and his or her historical moment, that the mystery of the human experience unfolds. That Samuel Johnson left behind enough material to allow us to peer into his own reckoning with history is a circumstance for which to be grateful.

AFTERWORD

~~~~~~~~~~~~~~~~~~~~~~~~~

IT IS POSSIBLE TO TRACE Samuel Johnson's descendants into the early twenty-first century. I began that quest in an effort to find living descendants, with the hope that they might share some family stories that would help round out the document-based narrative. No such luck, although somewhere out there is a Ulysses P. Malvan, Samuel Johnson's great-great-great-great-grandson, and if he would like to contact me, I would be over the moon.

Although unable to get in touch with living descendants, I still found the hunt for them worthwhile. Thanks to the miracle of searchable Census and other records through Ancestry.com, I was able to gather a good deal of information. What I learned helped put Samuel Johnson's story in context and also suggested the persistence of a set of Johnson-Malvin-Elkins family values. Among those values is a strong commitment to family. Samuel Johnson would have been happy to know that his grandchildren kept close ties with one another after both Lucy and Sandy Elkins died. The Census takers usually found at least two of them together in the same house in the 1870s, 1880s, and 1890s. In that era Lucy and Sandy's sons Jasper and Jerome owned a successful blacksmithing and wheelwright business on L Street in Washington, and it appears that Jerome taught his nephew the trade, for the nephew later became a wheelwright too.[1]

The next generation—Lucy and Sandy's grandchildren, Samuel Johnson's great-grandchildren—seem to have had a harder time of things. The apparent downturn in the family's fortunes coincided with the nadir of American race relations around the turn of the twentieth century. Many of Thomas Thornton Withers Malvin's children died in their infancy or youth, and a good number of that generation who survived had few or no children of their own. All three of Robina Elkins Cossey's Ohio-based children were childless into their forties (based on the latest Census records available).[2] The jobs that Johnson's descendants held in the 1910s, 1920s, and 1930s put them in the lower or middle class: waitstaff like their great-grandfather, a fireman at the gasworks, a secretary, a couple of clerks, a seamstress. Some of them had moved into the ranks of white-collar workers, but they all rented rather than owned the homes in which they lived, and often took in boarders to make ends meet or were themselves boarders in others' houses. Their lives were obscure, and their fates difficult to uncover. They did not form ties with important local elites, and they did not come to the attention of white patrons.[3]

One exception was Jasper's musician son, William C. Elkins, who along with his brothers Hanson and Henry headed to New York in the early twentieth century. They did not make it big, but William C. Elkins got close. He apparently supported himself as a working musician, and contributed in an important way to the birth of African American musical theater. (He too, however, did not own his home and his wife took in boarders.) Elkins performed in 1903 in the show *In Dahomey*, which was "the first full-length musical written and performed by blacks to be booked into a Broadway house."[4] Bert Williams and George Walker, the two leading African American performers in New York, produced and starred in the show in an effort to take control of the on-stage image of black people at a time when blackface minstrelsy was common. *In Dahomey* was a hit, and Williams and Walker chose Elkins to direct the choral music for their next show, *Abyssinia*, in 1906. William C. Elkins continued to perform and direct music for thirty years.[5]

Elkins's biggest contribution to American music and performance history came with the formation of the Elkins-Payne

Jubilee Singers, who sang African American religious music, an early form of gospel, and made a number of recordings in the 1920s. Listening to the Elkins-Payne Jubilee Singers on those old recordings, one senses that they, like other groups of that type, performed for white as well as black audiences. Jubilee singing started as a way to popularize black musical styles among white people and to raise money for Fisk University, the home base of the first jubilee singing group.[6] Like Williams and Walker's musical comedies, jubilee singing also provided a way to counter the images of the minstrel show and to present African American music that was not jokey or based on racial stereotypes.

The songs recorded by William C. Elkins's group reflect those values. They are clearly influenced by African American musical traditions, particularly in the way that Elkins arranged the harmonies. Paramount Records aimed the advertisements for these "race records" at black consumers, but the songs also possess a formalized quality that might have appealed to white people.[7] They are not the sounds of field workers or railroad linemen. Elkins chose songs designed to entice white listeners. A prominent example is "Silent Night"—the only documented recording by black singers before the 1940s of a traditional white Christmas carol.[8]

In singing for white audiences, Elkins lived very much in the tradition of his great-grandfather Samuel Johnson, who in his own way performed for white audiences and whose performance as a waiter in the tavern in Warrenton earned many accolades. Like his great-grandfather, William Elkins retained and asserted his own dignity even while orienting himself toward white eyes and ears. If Elkins sounded at all like his great-grandfather, then listening to him sing the lead on "You Must Shun Old Satan" brings us as close as we can get to Samuel Johnson in the flesh.[9]

There, in the flesh, lies another significant theme of the family's extended story. The color of one's skin continued to matter a lot for Johnson's descendants. One of his great-grandchildren, Hanson Webster Elkins, apparently decided that the only way to escape the burdens of color was actually to become white—perhaps something that Samuel Johnson had yearned to do. In 1942 when he registered for the draft, Hanson Elkins, William C. Elkins's younger brother, was listed as a white man with gray eyes and red hair. As he had been when he registered during the First World War in 1917, Hanson was large—tall and heavily built. His birthday and place of birth had not changed either. But his race had. Nothing could better underscore how much race was—and is—simultaneously substantive and slippery.

Another theme of Samuel Johnson's life and the lives of his descendants is the quest for upward mobility. Although most of Johnson's descendants did not succeed in moving upward, Garey Browne Jr., Edinborough's great-grandson and Samuel Johnson's great-great-great-grandson, lived a life notable enough to earn an obituary in the *Washington Post* in the year 2000. The *Post* described him as a juvenile court probation officer, a Korean War veteran, and a graduate of American University and Howard University, where he obtained a degree in social work. In his off time, he served as chairman of the Columbia Heights Boys Club. Like Samuel Johnson, Garey Browne Jr. was familiar with courts and their people, and held great respect for the law, as well as an abiding concern with children (although he had no children of his own). Browne was also a civil leader who earned respect from others; he served a term as mayor of Highland Beach, Florida, in 1979–81.[10] Browne seems to have lived a life less shaped by race than the lives of other Johnson descendants, but having been born in 1937 in Washington, D.C., he grew up at a time when black men were expected to step off the sidewalk if they saw a white woman approach.[11]

For all of Johnson's descendants, as for Johnson himself, race continued to operate not just as an idea or a legal reality, but as a fact of daily life that people themselves made and defined—in the interaction that took place when a black man cleared the sidewalk for a white woman, in the exchange between a black performer and white audience members in a New York theater, in the unrecorded dynamic between a white customer and her black seamstress, and in the turning of Hanson Webster Elkins from a black man to a white one. It is impossible to know whether Samuel Johnson would be more impressed by the persistence of race or by the depth of the differences that separate our time from his. We cannot ask him directly, so once again we are left to imagine. I think that he would be glad to see how far America has moved toward its ideal of equality, but that he would prod us in his gentle but determined and dignified way to do more, to go further, to not give up.

ACKNOWLEDGMENTS

ACKNOWLEDGMENTS SECTIONS, like Samuel Johnson's petitions to the Virginia legislature, tend to be formulaic. But I mean what I say as sincerely as he did. It really is a great pleasure to thank the many people who helped make this book. I will start with my parents, who first thought the story of Samuel Johnson was worth telling. To do so, I had to gather as much information on Johnson and his time and place as I could, a process I began in 2001 with the support of a faculty research grant from Hobart and William Smith Colleges. My colleagues there, especially Dan Singal, responded to my early thoughts on Johnson's story, and I am grateful for their encouragement.

Over the next decade, I received wonderful help from many people. Thank you to all those at the Afro-American Historical Association of Fauquier County, especially Karen Hughes White, who answered some crucial questions that arose as the manuscript neared completion. Jane Butler, also of the AAHA, graciously helped me gather information on Warrenton's free black residents and sent photocopies of useful documents. In the courthouse at Fauquier County, the records room staff delivered and copied some crucial records during my 2001 research trip, and later, deputy clerks Phyllis Scott and Kathy Brown helped tie up some loose ends. Scott, in particular, went beyond the call of duty on an ultimately fruitless search through the clerk's loose papers. On a final trip to Warrenton in the summer of 2011, I was lucky to meet with Frances Allshouse, director of the Fauquier Historical Society, who shared many useful resources. I also want to thank those who provided (free) lodging and good companionship on my research trips: Blair Pogue and Dwight Zscheile in Fauquier and Barbara Smith in Richmond.

For helping to track down information on jubilee singing, I am grateful to my San Francisco State colleague Dean Suzuki, who also took a listen and helped me understand what I was hearing. Paul Ellison and Lee Hildebrand also aided in my search for information on the Elkins-Payne Jubilee Singers. Crucial research assistance came from Michael Caires, who did some tedious but important work very well, the fruits of which appear in chapter 4. Chris Kolbe of the Library of Virginia checked some details for me and helped me obtain permission to use images from the library's collection. Thank you, Chris.

I wrote this book on and off over many years. When the project was on, it was in large measure thanks to two full-time, one-semester leaves from teaching at San Francisco State University—a Presidential Award in the fall of 2006 and a sabbatical leave in the fall of 2010. Thank you, President Corrigan, for supporting scholarship even in the midst of draconian budget cuts. An advance from the University of Georgia Press allowed me to take a partial leave from teaching in the spring of 2009, which helped me to get some momentum going again after one of the off periods.

I shared the work in progress with a number of people, all of whom provided helpful feedback. Thanks to Melvin Ely, Joshua Rothman, and T. Stephen Whitman, who commented on papers that I delivered at professional conferences, and to Ellen Eslinger, who generously shared her paper from one of those conferences. In later communications, Mel prodded me to rethink the use of the term "white negroes"; I am deeply grateful to him. Colleagues and graduate students at San Francisco State offered their usual sharp criticism and encouragement in a colloquium discussion of the first chapter of this book, as did Manisha Sinha in her comments on that early partial draft. I feel especially thankful for the efforts and insights of those who read the complete manuscript. My mother-in-law, Doris Wolf, and my San Francisco State colleagues Dawn Mabalon and Sarah Curtis provided comments that helped sharpen the manuscript and improve its readability. Sarah, in particular, saved me from a number of illogical statements. On behalf of the University of Georgia Press, Douglas Egerton and Richard Newman read a full draft and gave me excellent suggestions, most of which I have silently and shamelessly passed off as my own insights and knowledge. Thanks, guys! Even after all that feedback, a number of kinks remained. Thanks to my mom and dad and to Merryl Sloane for ironing them out in the copyediting process.

This book is being published as part of the Race in the Atlantic World series mostly because I wanted to work with the wonderful editors of that series. Thanks to Richard Newman, Patrick Rael, and Manisha Sinha for inviting me on board. It was Derek Krissoff of the University of Georgia Press who first contacted me about participating in the series, and he has been a pleasure to work with—flexible, responsive, and encouraging. Indeed, everyone at the press has been delightful.

When, in the mid-1990s, I first discovered Samuel Johnson in the archives of the Library of Virginia, I was inspired by his determination—a fitting theme for a graduate student, as I was then. After I became a mother, I found myself more drawn to Johnson's commitment to and concern for his family. Deep thanks to Sven, Matthew, and Ezra for helping me to understand what it means to make a family, and for thinking that it is cool that I have been working on a book. Now that the book is done, I offer it as a gift to them, and to you, the reader, without whom the act of writing history will not have had much meaning.

NOTES

ABBREVIATIONS

AAHAFC   Afro-American Historical Association of Fauquier County

Census   U.S. Census population schedules, National Archives and Records Administration, microfilm

CV 1849   *The Code of Virginia* . . . (Richmond: William F. Ritchie, 1849)

Deeds   Deed Book, Library of Virginia, Richmond, Va., 23219, microfilm

FC   Fauquier County

FCMB   Fauquier County Court Minute Books, Library of Virginia, Richmond, Va., 23219, microfilm

FN/Sl   Free Negro/Slave

Hening   William Waller Hening, *The Statutes at Large: Being a Collection of All the Laws of Virginia from the First Session of the Legislature, in the Year 1619.* 13 vols. (Richmond: Samuel Pleasants, 1809–1823)

LP   Virginia General Assembly, Legislative Petitions of the General Assembly, State Government Records Collection, Library of Virginia, Richmond, Va., 23219

LVA   Library of Virginia, Richmond, Va., 23219

RCV 1819   *The Revised Code of the Laws of Virginia: Being a Collection of All Such Acts of the General Assembly . . . as Are Now in Force* (Richmond: Thomas Ritchie, 1819)

RCV 1833   *Supplement to the Revised Code of the Laws of Virginia: Being a Collection of All the Acts of the General Assembly, . . . Passed since the Year 1819* . . . (Richmond: Samuel Shepherd, 1833)

RFN   *Fauquier County, Virginia, Register of Free Negros, 1817–1865*, abstracted and indexed by Karen King Ibrahim, Karen Hughes White, and Courtney Gaskins (Lovettesville, Va.: Willow Bend, 1996)

Shepherd   Samuel Shepherd, *The Statutes at Large of Virginia: From October Session 1792, to December Session 1806, Inclusive, in Three Volumes (New Series), Being a Continuation of Hening.* 3 vols. (Richmond: Samuel Shepherd, 1835–1836; rpt., New York: AMS, 1970)

SJP 1811   Virginia General Assembly, Legislative Petitions of the General Assembly, Sam's Petition, 13 Dec. 1811, Fauquier County, State Government Records Collection, Library of Virginia, Richmond, Va., 23219

SJP 1815   Virginia General Assembly, Legislative Petitions of the General Assembly, Samuel Johnson's Petition, 16 Dec. 1815, Fauquier County, State Government Records Collection, Library of Virginia, Richmond, Va., 23219

SJP 1820   Virginia General Assembly, Legislative Petitions of the General Assembly, Samuel Johnston Petition, 14 Dec. 1820, Fauquier County, State Government Records Collection, Library of Virginia, Richmond, Va., 23219

SJP 1822   Virginia General Assembly, Legislative Petitions of the General Assembly, Sam Johnson's Petition, 17 Dec. 1822, Fauquier County, State Government Records Collection, Library of Virginia, Richmond, Va., 23219

SJP 1823   Virginia General Assembly, Legislative Petitions of the

General Assembly, Sam Johnson's Petition, 4 Dec. 1823, Fauquier County, State Government Records Collection, Library of Virginia, Richmond, Va., 23219

SJP 1824   Virginia General Assembly, Legislative Petitions of the General Assembly, Samuel Johnson's Petition, 4 Dec. 1824, Fauquier County, State Government Records Collection, Library of Virginia, Richmond, Va., 23219

SJP 1826   Virginia General Assembly, Legislative Petitions of the General Assembly, Samuel Johnston Petition, 7 Dec. 1826, Fauquier County, State Government Records Collection, Library of Virginia, Richmond, Va., 23219

SJP 1828   Virginia General Assembly, Legislative Petitions of the General Assembly, Petition of Sam'l Johnston, 5 Dec. 1828, Fauquier County, State Government Records Collection, Library of Virginia, Richmond, Va., 23219

SJP 1835   Virginia General Assembly, Legislative Petitions of the General Assembly, Sam Johnson's Petition, 19 Jan. 1835, Fauquier County, State Government Records Collection, Library of Virginia, Richmond, Va., 23219

SJP 1837   Virginia General Assembly, Legislative Petitions of the General Assembly, Petition of Sam Johnson, 25 Jan. 1837, Fauquier County, State Government Records Collection, Library of Virginia, Richmond, Va., 23219

CHAPTER ONE. *A New Birth of Freedom*

1. Notation of Richard Brent deed of manumission to Samuel Johnson, 25 Aug. 1812, FCMB; Richard Brent deed of manumission to Samuel Johnson, 2 Aug. 1812, FC Deeds 18:474.

2. The 1810 U.S. Census summary gives a total Virginia population of 974,622, with 392,518 slaves and 30,570 nonwhite free persons.

3. The classic account of the free black experience in the United States is Ira Berlin's *Slaves without Masters: The Free Negro in the Antebellum*

South (New York: New Press, 1974). Melvin Patrick Ely has challenged Berlin's characterization of free blacks as masterless slaves in *Israel on the Appomattox: A Southern Experiment in Black Freedom from the 1790s through the Civil War* (New York: Knopf, 2004), which like this book relies on local records. Ely argues that masters' sense of dominance and their confidence in the slave system allowed them to grant free blacks a surprising amount of latitude.

4. Fauquier County Bicentennial Committee, *Fauquier County, Virginia* (Warrenton, Va.: Fauquier County Bicentennial Committee, 1959), 78.

5. The geography of Warrenton comes from an 1840 map in citizens petition, 19 Jan. 1841, FC, LP (oversized). There is every reason to believe that the main streets of 1840 also existed in 1812. Warrenton's 1819–20 businesses are listed in *Fauquier County*, 124–26.

6. *Fauquier County*, 78.

7. The Warrenton *Jeffersonian*, 23 May 1840 and 20 Mar. 1841. Today, Fauquier County is part bedroom community to Washington, D.C., and part horse country. In the year 2010 Fauquier had 65,203 residents, 8 percent of whom were African American. U.S. Census Bureau QuickFacts, http://quickfacts.census.gov/qfd/states/51/51061.html.

8. In the 1810 U.S. Census, Fauquier County had 22,689 people, of whom 10,361 were enslaved; Charles City County had 5,186, of whom 3,023 were enslaved; Greenbrier had 5,914, of whom 494 were enslaved.

9. Paul Lovejoy, *Transformations in Slavery: A History of Slavery in Africa*, 2nd ed. (Cambridge: Cambridge University Press, 2000); Patrick Manning, *Slavery and African Life: Occidental, Oriental, and African Slave Trades* (Cambridge: Cambridge University Press, 1990); and for part of the story of the slave trade to Virginia, Stephanie E. Smallwood, *Saltwater Slavery: A Middle Passage from Africa to American Diaspora* (Cambridge, Mass.: Harvard University Press, 2007).

10. In the mid- to late eighteenth-century Tidewater and Piedmont areas of Virginia, well over half of all families owned slaves, according to Allan Kulikoff, *Tobacco and Slaves: The Development of Southern Cultures in the Chesapeake, 1680–1800* (Chapel Hill: Published for the Institute of Early American History and Culture by University of North Carolina Press, 1986), 137, 154. In Fauquier County in 1810, 59 percent of white

households held at least one slave, and the average number of slaves per slaveholding household was 7.75, based on my sampling of every fifth household listed in the 1810 U.S. Census for Fauquier County.

11. Ira Berlin, *Many Thousands Gone: The First Two Centuries of Slavery in North America* (Cambridge, Mass.: Belknap, 1998), 114–15; John Kelly Thornton, *Africa and Africans in the Making of the Atlantic World, 1400–1800*, 2nd ed. (Cambridge: Cambridge University Press, 1998), 154–61.

12. The Atlantic Slave Trade database, estimates of disembarkation, http://www.slavevoyages.org/tast/assessment/estimates.faces; Edmund Morgan, *American Slavery, American Freedom: The Ordeal of Colonial Virginia* (New York: Norton, 1975), chs. 15–16; Berlin, *Many Thousands Gone*, chs. 1, 5; Philip D. Morgan, *Slave Counterpoint: Black Culture in the Eighteenth-Century Chesapeake and Lowcountry* (Chapel Hill: Published for the Omohundro Institute of Early American History and Culture, by University of North Carolina Press, 1998), 59, 61, 164–70.

13. Morgan, *Slave Counterpoint*, 61, 79–85.

14. Johnson's date of birth is from RFN, entry 3.

15. Samuel Johnson, "Taxation No Tyranny" (1775), http://www.samueljohnson.com/tnt.html.

16. Morgan, *Slave Counterpoint*, 98–101.

17. Arthur Zilversmit, *The First Emancipation: The Abolition of Slavery in the North* (Chicago: University of Chicago Press, 1967); Don E. Fehrenbacher, *The Slaveholding Republic: An Account of the United States Government's Relations to Slavery*, completed and ed. by Ward McAfee (New York: Oxford University Press, 2001), 138–42. The federal law could not be enacted until 1808 according to Article I, section 9, of the U.S. Constitution.

18. Eva Sheppard Wolf, *Race and Liberty in the New Nation: Emancipation in Virginia from the Revolution to Nat Turner's Rebellion* (Baton Rouge: Louisiana State University Press, 2006), ch. 1.

19. "Bright mulatto" is from RFN, entry 3.

20. RFN, entries 1–117, covering the period 1817–29. In Lancaster County too, a majority (about two-thirds) of those in the Register of Free Negroes from 1803 to 1831 were "mulatto," "tawny," "bright," or "yellow." Lancaster Co. Register of Free Negroes, 1803–60, LVA (microfilm).

Although not all free black Virginians registered, the true number of "mulattos" is almost certainly above 50 percent.

21. Walter Johnson, *Soul by Soul: Life inside the Antebellum Slave Market* (Cambridge, Mass.: Harvard University Press, 1999), 137–40.

22. SJP 1811.

23. Henry Wiencek, *An Imperfect God: George Washington, His Slaves, and the Creation of America* (New York: Farrar, Straus & Giroux, 2003), 68.

24. Rhys Isaac, *The Transformation of Virginia, 1740–1790* (New York: Norton, 1982), 88–98.

25. *Virginia Gazette and General Advertiser* (Richmond), 28 Sept. 1791; Wolf, *Race and Liberty*, ch. 2, app. A; certificate of Edmd. Brooke, 6 June 1792, FC Deeds 14:874; Enock Foley deed of manumission to Fanny Davis, 22 Dec. 1800, ibid.:873; Gideon Johnson deed of manumission to Judy Patience, 26 Mar. 1800, ibid.:705.

26. *Fauquier County*, 73, 75; FC Personal Property Tax Records, 1801, LVA (microfilm); notation re: Edward Digges Jr., 25 Aug. 1817, FCMB (for evidence of Digges's mill).

27. "A Richmond Paper of Sept. 12," as printed in *Gazette of the United States*, 18 Sept. 1800.

28. Ibid.; *Philadelphia Gazette*, 27 Sept. 1800.

29. Douglas R. Egerton, *Gabriel's Rebellion: The Virginia Slave Conspiracies of 1800 and 1802* (Chapel Hill: University of North Carolina Press, 1993), 109.

30. *Gazette of the United States*, 18 Sept. 1800. The *Gazette of the United States* was a Federalist, and very much anti-Jefferson, newspaper.

31. SJP 1811; Richmond *Enquirer*, 12 Sept. 1807.

32. SJP 1811.

33. *Prince William Reliquary* 2, no. 2 (Apr. 2003): 30; "Richard Brent," in Sara B. Bearss, John T. Kneebone, J. Jefferson Looney, Brent Tarter, and Sandra Gioia Treadway, eds., *Dictionary of Virginia Biography*, vol. 2 (Richmond: Library of Virginia, 2001), 218–19.

34. Wolf, *Race and Liberty*, 63–66.

35. John Love bill of sale to Samuel Johnson, 24 Nov. 1818, FC Deeds 23:62; county expenses, 27 June 1815, FCMB.

36. In 1819 the county court set the tavern rates so that a warm dinner

with a toddy and spirits cost fifty cents. Based on that pricing, Johnson's tips were probably a few pennies or perhaps a nickel at a time. Tavern rates, 28 June 1819, FCMB.

37. Citizens petition, 2 Dec. 1800, King and Queen Co., LP.

38. "A Bill to prevent the partial emancipation of Slaves except in certain cases and under certain restrictions," 28 Dec. 1803, House of Delegates Rough Bills, LVA archives.

39. "A Bill to prevent the emancipation of slaves within this Commonwealth," 8 Jan. 1805, House of Delegates Rough Bills, LVA archives.

40. SJP 1815. Sam Jr.'s year of birth is inferred from Lucy's birth year of 1805, according to Lucy Malvin petition, 3 Jan. 1838, FC, LP. Sam was older, and the typical spacing between children was about two years.

41. Lucinda's petition, 27 Nov. 1813, King George Co., in *Race, Slavery and Free Blacks*, ser. 1: *Petitions to Southern Legislatures, 1777–1867* (Bethesda, Md.: University Publications of America, 1998), microfilm ed., reel 17, accession 11681303; John H. Russell, *The Free Negro in Virginia* (Baltimore, Md.: Johns Hopkins University Press, 1913; rpt., New York: Negro Universities Press, 1969), 76.

42. Petition of Stephen Bias [Bears?], 14 Feb. 1839, Albemarle Co., LP.

43. Lucy was born in 1805. See n. 40, above.

44. SJP 1811. In transcribing this and other documents, I have modified punctuation slightly for readability.

45. I have tried to match the handwriting on the petition to that of people whose identity I know, but with no luck.

46. 1820 Census, Warrenton, Va.

47. Citizens testimonial, SJP 1811.

48. Edward Digges's certificate, 12 Jan. 1812, included in SJP 1811.

49. Wolf, *Race and Liberty*, 141n18.

50. The estimated number of petitioners comes from a search of the Legislative Petitions database, Library of Virginia, http://www.lva .virginia.gov/public/guides/petitions/petitionsSearch.asp. The fraction that succeeded is estimated from the petitions listed in H. J. Eckenrode, *A Calendar Of Legislative Petitions, Arranged by Counties: Accomac-Bedford* (Richmond: Davis Bottom, 1908), and also from an incomplete collection of petitions I examined from Charles City, Chesterfield, Fauquier,

Halifax, Lancaster, and Powhatan counties. Out of this sample of fifty petitions, eighteen were rejected outright, five were found reasonable but failed to become law, and only four definitively led to bills being passed on behalf of the petitioners. Most of the rest were found reasonable, but either they did not lead to bills being drawn and passed or their ultimate fates are unclear.

51. The back of the petition includes the note, "bill drawn." SJP 1811.

52. John Scott to William Poindexter, n.d., SJP 1811.

53. Richard Brent deed of manumission to Samuel Johnson, 2 Aug. 1812, FC Deeds 18:474.

54. Ibid.; notation regarding Richard Brent deed of manumission to Samuel Johnson, 25 Aug. 1812, FCMB.

CHAPTER TWO. *Among an Anomalous Population*

1. SJP 1815.

2. Old & others petition, 16 Dec. 1809, Amelia Co., LP; John H. Russell, *The Free Negro in Virginia* (Baltimore, Md.: Johns Hopkins University Press, 1913; rpt., New York: Negro Universities Press, 1969), 77, 77n139.

3. Philip J. Schwarz, "Emancipators, Protectors, and Anomalies: Free Black Slaveowners in Virginia," *Virginia Magazine of History and Biography* 95, no. 3 (July 1987): 317–38.

4. SJP 1815.

5. RCV 1819, ch. III, sec. 62; also see Eva Sheppard Wolf, *Race and Liberty in the New Nation: Emancipation in Virginia from the Revolution to Nat Turner's Rebellion* (Baton Rouge: Louisiana State University Press, 2006), 134–35.

6. Motions of Barnett Toliver and Betsy Davis, 29 Oct., 25 Nov., and 23 Dec. 1816, 27 Jan. and 25 Feb. 1817, FCMB; case of Barnett Toliver, 25 Mar. 1817, ibid.; case of Jack and Hannah and their children, 27 Oct. 1817, ibid.

7. Motions of Barnett Toliver and Betsy Davis, 29 Oct., 25 Nov., and 23 Dec. 1816, 27 Jan. and 25 Feb. 1817, FCMB; motions of Betsey [*sic*] Davis, 25 Mar., 26 May, 23 June, and 28 July 1817, ibid.; RFN, entry 190.

8. RCV 1819, ch. III, sec. 62.

9. Sharon Braslaw Sundue, *Industrious in Their Stations: Young People at Work in Urban America, 1720–1810* (Charlottesville: University of Virginia Press, 2009), 34, 184.

10. Certificate of Ann Norris, SJP 1835.

11. Exhibit (image 20 in the online version), *Fant v. Elkins*, 1847-052, FC Chancery Court Records, FC Circuit Court Records Room, Warrenton, and http://www.lva.virginia.gov/chancery/case_detail .asp?CFN=061-1847-052.

12. Henry Fitzhugh and Berkley Ward resignation of committee membership, 23 May 1820, FCMB; Ann A. Norris declaration of guardian, 29 Nov. 1820, ibid.

13. *Samuel Johnson v. Thaddeus Norris*, 26 Mar. and 25 Nov. 1818, 23 Mar., 27 Aug., and 23 Nov. 1819, FCMB; certificate of Ann Norris, SJP 1835.

14. *Samuel Johnson v. Thaddeus Norris*, 26 Mar. 1818, FCMB.

15. The lack of extant records is according to Phyllis Scott, deputy clerk of Fauquier County, 14 Dec. 2010.

16. John Love bill of sale to Samuel Johnson, 24 Nov. 1818, FC Deeds 23:62.

17. The well is mentioned in an 1822 deed, and it is possible, but not likely, that it had not yet been dug in 1818. Indenture between John A. W. Smith and Maria L. his wife, and Samuel Johnston, Nov. 1822, FC Deeds 26:426.

18. Fauquier County Bicentennial Committee, *Fauquier County, Virginia* (Warrenton: Fauquier County Bicentennial Committee), 125.

19. 1820 Census, Fauquier County, p. 122.

20. Russell, *Free Negro*, 112–13; Hening 8:393.

21. For more discussion of this point, see Kathleen M. Brown, *Good Wives, Nasty Wenches, and Anxious Patriarchs: Gender, Race, and Power in Colonial Virginia* (Chapel Hill: Published for the Omohundro Institute of Early American History and Culture, by University of North Carolina Press, 1996), 116–20.

22. Hening 4:126.

23. Ibid. 3:252; Shepherd 1:122–30. Sally Hemings's grandmother was African, but both her father and grandfather were white. See Joshua D. Rothman, *Notorious in the Neighborhood: Sex and Families across the Color*

Line in Virginia, 1787–1861 (Chapel Hill: University of North Carolina Press, 2003), 18–19, 46–47.

24. Shepherd 3:274.

25. Russell, *Free Negro*, 117; Hening 5:244–45. From 1732, free black Virginians could testify in court only in capital cases concerning slaves; Hening 4:327.

26. Hening 12:182; Shepherd 1:123. One positive change was the 1788 repeal of the act making it manslaughter only (not murder) to kill a slave while punishing him or her. Hening 12:681.

27. Shepherd 1:125, 127, 128; Hening 11:40; Shepherd 3:124.

28. *Parks v. Hewlett*, 1838, 14 Grattan 251, cited in Russell, *Free Negro*, 89.

29. Hening 22:531. The act calls people who steal the children of free blacks and "mulattos," "evil disposed persons" and provides severe punishment: "death without benefit of clergy."

30. Indenture between John A. W. Smith and Maria L. his wife, and Samuel Johnston, Nov. 1822, FC Deeds 26:426.

31. The poll tax was rescinded in 1788, but counties still levied taxes on "tithables," or adult male workers. Hening 12:413; Russell, *Free Negro*, 112–14; Robin L. Einhorn, *American Taxation, American Slavery* (Chicago: University of Chicago Press, 2006), 37–52.

32. FC Personal Property Tax Books, 1815–44, LVA (microfilm).

33. Ralph Ellison, *Invisible Man* (New York: Random House, 1952).

34. Thomas Jefferson to Edward Coles, 25 Aug. 1814, in Henry S. Randall, *The Life of Thomas Jefferson* (New York: Derby & Jackson, 1858), 3:644.

35. Citizens petition, 2 Dec. 1800, King and Queen Co., LP.

36. Thomas Robertson speech, Virginia House of Delegates, 15 Jan. 1806, in *Virginia Argus*, 17 Jan. 1806.

37. Citizens petition, 16 Dec. 1831, Northampton Co., LP.

38. Ibid.; James Sidbury, *Ploughshares into Swords: Race, Rebellion, and Identity in Gabriel's Virginia, 1730–1810* (Cambridge: Cambridge University Press, 1997); Tommy L. Bogger, *Free Blacks in Norfolk, Virginia, 1790–1860: The Darker Side of Freedom* (Charlottesville: University of Virginia Press, 1997).

39. Land area from U.S. Census Bureau QuickFacts, http://quickfacts.census.gov/qfd/states/51/51061.html. Fauquier has not changed size since the 1820s.

40. 1820 Census, Fauquier County.

41. Wolf, *Race and Liberty*, 117, 119–20; Shepherd 1:23, 2:301; RCV 1819, ch. 111, sec. 67. For examples of those who appeared in court to certify their right to freedom, see appearance of Winny and Nancy Grayson, 29 Aug. 1815, FCMB; and appearance of Daniel, Betty, and Nancy, 28 Oct. 1817, ibid.

42. RFN, entry 3. Of the twelve black heads of household in Warrenton named in the 1820 Census (one of the eleven families had two heads of household), only three people besides Samuel Johnson have entries in the Register of Free Negroes: Nace Piles, Sally Grayson, and Fanny Levers.

43. RFN, entries 1, 2, 12. Nace's last name is Pile in the Register of Free Negroes, but Piles in the Census.

44. RFN, entries 1, 2, 5, and 11. I am working on a statistical evaluation of the data on bodily marks and intend to publish the results in a forthcoming journal article.

45. *Commonwealth v. Stone*, FN/Sl Ended Causes 1854-017, FC Clerk's Loose Papers, photocopy at AAHAFC. The case began on 1 Nov. and ended 27 Nov. 1854.

46. Alexandria *Gazette and Daily Advertiser*, 3 June 1817; Richmond *Enquirer*, 5 July 1822.

47. Citizens petition, 23 Jan. 1830, FC, LP.

48. *Commonwealth v. N. Piles*, FN/Sl Commonwealth Cause from Ended Causes 1829-006, FC Clerk's Loose Papers, photocopy at AAHAFC; RFN, entry 1 ("simple unmeaning countenance").

49. Rothman, *Notorious in the Neighborhood*.

50. Grand jury presentment against Philip Hughes and Lucy Edwards, March Court 1816, FN/Sl Commonwealth Cause from Ended Causes 1816-020, FC Clerk's Loose Papers, photocopy at AAHAFC.

51. RFN, entry 607.

52. Rothman, *Notorious in the Neighborhood*.

53. Shepherd 1:122–30, esp. 126; Sidbury, *Ploughshares into Swords*, 192–94; Douglas R. Egerton, *Gabriel's Rebellion: The Virginia Slave*

Conspiracies of 1800 and 1802 (Chapel Hill: University of North Carolina Press, 1993), 25–27.

54. Ira Berlin, *Slaves without Masters: The Free Negro in the Antebellum South* (New York: New Press, 1974).

CHAPTER THREE. *Petitioning for Freedom in an Era of Slavery*

1. Even emancipating them during his life did not guarantee their freedom, since the 1792 slave code included a provision that emancipated slaves could be sold to pay off debts contracted by the owner before the date of emancipation. Shepherd 1:128.

2. Thomas Marshall speech, 6 Feb. 1832, in Richmond *Enquirer*, 14 Feb. 1832.

3. The original provision in the 1806 law was that the funds from the sale of free black illegal residents should go to aid the poor. After the establishment in 1810 of the Literary Fund, such monies were funneled there. Shepherd 3:252; Foney G. Mullins, "A History of the Literary Fund as a Funding Source for Free Public Education in the Commonwealth of Virginia," Ed.D. diss., Virginia Polytechnic Institute, 2001.

4. John G. Joynes petition, 31 Dec. 1834, Accomack Co., LP.

5. Brenda E. Stevenson, *Life in Black and White: Family and Community in the Slave South* (New York: Oxford University Press, 1996), 269.

6. Frederick Co. Minute Book, 1830–34, 3 Sept. 1833, p. 446, cited in Ellen Eslinger, "Free Black Residency under Virginia's 1806 Manumission Law: The Lower Shenandoah Valley," paper delivered at the Virginia Forum, Winchester, Va., Apr. 2006.

7. Douglas R. Egerton, *Death or Liberty: African Americans and Revolutionary America* (New York: Oxford University Press, 2009), 58–60, 103–10; Loren Schweninger, ed., *The Southern Debate over Slavery*, vol. 1: *Petitions to Southern Legislatures, 1778–1864* (Urbana: University of Illinois Press, 2001), xxi–xxvi. Also see ch. 1, n. 50, above.

8. SJP 1820.

9. FC Personal Property Tax Records, 1814–44, LVA (microfilm).

10. SJP 1823. The Fauquier County clerk's website notes, "A law requiring the statewide recording of births and deaths was passed by the Virginia General Assembly on April 11, 1853 and continued until 1896

when legislation repealed the recording provisions. There are no birth and death records prior to 1853 and no records from 1897 to June 14, 1912, either at the county or state level." http://www.fauquiercounty.gov/government /departments/circuitcourt/index.cfm?action=recordroom.

11. RCV 1819, ch. III, sec. 62.

12. SJP 1822.

13. In the 1820s most states still operated under the laws of coverture, in which a woman's property became her husband's when she married. Anything she earned was considered his, and he was understood to be the household's representative to the outside world.

14. SJP 1822; RCV 1819, ch. III, sec. 62.

15. SJP 1823; James D. Watkinson, "'Fit Objects of Charity': Community, Race, Faith, and Welfare in Antebellum Lancaster County, Virginia, 1817–1860," *Journal of the Early Republic* 21, no. 1 (Spring 2001): 41–70.

16. SJP 1823.

17. Citizens testimonial, SJP 1823; Warrenton *Gazette*, 4 Nov. 1826; 1830 Census, Warrenton. For Scott as commonwealth's attorney, see FCMB, 1815–18.

18. *Commonwealth v. Richard W. Chichester*, 28 Mar. and 25 Apr. 1815, FCMB.

19. SJP 1824.

20. John Shackelford and J. C. Gibson notes, SJP 1824. I have not been able to find out much more about Shackelford and Gibson. This John Shackelford may have been the same as John Shackleford, commonwealth's attorney of neighboring Culpeper Co., who was married to Lucy Tutt, a niece of Revolutionary leader Edmund Pendleton. Raleigh Travers Green and Philip Slaughter, *Genealogical Notes on Culpeper Co., Virginia* (copyright by BiblioBazaar), 100 (viewed on Google Books).

21. SJP 1824.

22. SJP 1826.

23. Lucy Malvin petition, 3 Jan. 1838, FC, LP; RFN, entry 77.

24. SJP 1835.

25. *Millon v. Malvin*, FN/Sl Ended Causes 1832-038, FC Clerk's Loose Papers, FC Circuit Court Records Room, Warrenton.

26. Examining Court for Fielding Sinclair, 19 Sept. 1818, FCMB.

27. Complaint of Spencer Malvin, 26 Oct. 1818, ibid.; *Commonwealth v. Fielding Sinclair*, 25 Nov. 1818, ibid.; *Malvin v. Sinclair*, FN/Sl Ended Causes 1818-028, FC Clerk's Loose Papers, FC Circuit Court Records Room, Warrenton; Overseers of the Poor re: Spencer Malvin, 26 Nov. 1818 and 22 Mar. 1819, FCMB.

28. FC Deeds 29:105.

29. John K. Gott, *Fauquier County, Virginia, Marriage Bonds: 1759–1854 and Marriage Returns: 1785–1848* (Bowie, Md.: Heritage, 1989), 129.

30. SJP 1826.

31. Ibid.; Edward Digges will, 27 Oct. 1818, FC Wills 7:223–24 (for evidence that Sarah D. Digges was Edward's daughter).

32. Fauquier County Bicentennial Committee, *Fauquier County, Virginia* (Warrenton, Va.: Fauquier County Bicentennial Committee, 1959), 125; Richmond *Enquirer*, 26 Sept. 1826; SJP 1826; Biographical Directory of the U.S. Congress, http://bioguide.congress.gov/biosearch /biosearch.asp.

33. The 1820 Census, Orange Co., shows that Philip Pendleton Barbour owned forty-six slaves, while the 1820 Census, Culpeper Co., shows that John Strode Barbour owned eighteen. For their votes, see *Journal of the House of Representatives of the United States, 1828–1829* (6 Jan. 1829): 126–28, http://memory.loc.gov/ammem/amlaw/lawhome .html.

34. RCV 1819, ch. III, sec. 61.

35. The RFN shows no entry for Lucy under any of her last names.

36. SJP 1828.

37. *Charles & al. v. Hunnicutt*, 5 Call 311, Oct. 1804, accessed through LexisNexis.

38. Glover Moore, *The Missouri Controversy, 1819–1821* (Lexington: University of Kentucky Press, 1953), 45–46; Eva Sheppard Wolf, *Race and Liberty: Emancipation in Virginia from the Revolution to Nat Turner's Rebellion* (Baton Rouge: Louisiana State University Press, 2006), 173.

39. Wolf, *Race and Liberty*, 156–57.

40. For early examples, see Richmond *Enquirer*, 25 and 29 Dec. 1819 and 23 Dec. 1820.

41. Douglas R. Egerton, *He Shall Go Out Free: The Lives of Denmark*

Vesey (Madison, Wis.: Madison House, 1999), 135–36, and personal communication with the author.

42. Richmond *Enquirer*, 26 Sept. 1826.

CHAPTER FOUR. *Visions of Rebellion*

1. Stephen B. Oates, *The Fires of Jubilee: Nat Turner's Fierce Rebellion* (New York: Harper & Row, 1975; rpt., Harper Perennial, 1990), 41.

2. See Richard S. Newman, *The Transformation of American Abolitionism: Fighting Slavery in the Early Republic* (Chapel Hill: University of North Carolina Press, 2002), 128–29.

3. U.S. Census Summary, table 4: Population, 1790–1990, http://www.census.gov/population/www/censusdata/files/table-4.pdf.

4. *Annals of Congress*, House of Representatives, 14th Cong., 2nd sess., 4 Feb. 1817, p. 854, http://memory.loc.gov/ammem/amlaw/lwac.html.

5. L. H. Butterfield, "The Jubilee of Independence, July 4, 1826," *Virginia Magazine of History and Biography* 61, no. 2 (Apr. 1953): 119–40; Richmond *Enquirer*, 6 Sept. 1825; Andrew Burstein, *America's Jubilee* (New York: Knopf, 2001), 8, 30.

6. Richmond *Enquirer*, 6 Sept. 1825.

7. 1810 Census, St. Ann's, Albemarle Co., Va. (Monroe); 1820 Census, Washington, D.C., Ward 1 (Monroe); 1820 Census, Richmond, Va., Monroe Ward (Marshall); 1820 Census, Warrenton, Va. (Moore). These figures might have differed slightly in 1825.

8. He is, however, mentioned in John H. Russell, *The Free Negro in Virginia* (Baltimore, Md.: Johns Hopkins University Press, 1913; rpt., New York: Negro Universities Press, 1969), 131–32, and his 1820 petition appears in Loren Schweninger, ed., *The Southern Debate over Slavery*, vol. 1: *Petitions to Southern Legislatures, 1778–1864* (Urbana: University of Illinois Press, 2001), 65–66.

9. 1830 Census, Warrenton, p. 476; Samuel Malvin entry, 1860 U.S. Census mortality schedule, Washington, D.C., found in "U.S. Federal Census Mortality Schedules, 1850–1880," *Ancestry.com*, 2005; *Fant v. Elkins*, 1847-052, FC Chancery Court Records, FC Circuit Court Records Room, Warrenton, and http://www.lva.virginia.gov/chancery/case_detail.asp?CFN=061-1847-052.

10. 1830 Census, Warrenton, p. 476.

11. Alexander Keyssar, *The Right to Vote: The Contested History of Democracy in the United States* (New York: Basic, 2000), 29, table A.2.

12. See John Cooke's speech in *Proceedings and Debates of the Virginia State Convention of 1829–30, to Which Are Subjoined, the New Constitution of Virginia, and the Votes of the People* (Richmond: Printed by Samuel Shepherd for Ritchie and Cook, 1830), 54–62; and Dickson D. Bruce Jr., *The Rhetoric of Conservatism: The Virginia Convention of 1829–30 and the Conservative Tradition in the South* (San Marino, Calif.: Huntington Library, 1982), 18–26.

13. *Proceedings and Debates*, 3–4.

14. David W. Conroy, *In Public Houses: Drink and the Revolution of Authority in Colonial Massachusetts* (Chapel Hill: University of North Carolina Press, published for the Omohundro Institute of Early American History and Culture, 1995), 180n38, 233–36; Charles G. Steffen, "Newspapers for Free: The Economies of Newspaper Circulation in the Early Republic," *Journal of the Early Republic* 23, no. 3 (Autumn 2003): 381–419.

15. *Proceedings and Debates*, 149.

16. Ibid., 68.

17. In the end, the convention did modify the suffrage requirements, but still did not provide for universal white male suffrage and continued to bar free blacks and all women from the vote. Virginia Constitution of 1830, Article III, sec. 14, ibid., 900.

18. Oates, *Fires of Jubilee*, 47.

19. Ibid., 70–77, quotation on 70.

20. Ibid., 78, 85–90.

21. Ibid., 91–99.

22. Ibid., 99, 116–25; Patrick H. Breen, "Nat Turner's Revolt: Rebellion and Response in Southampton County, Virginia," Ph.D. diss., University of Georgia, 2005, pp. 157–71, 245, 256–74. Oates writes that about twice as many blacks as whites were killed in the aftermath of Turner's Rebellion, but Breen convincingly shows that the number was much smaller.

23. Adam Rothman, *Slave Country: American Expansion and the Origins of the Deep South* (Cambridge, Mass.: Harvard University Press, 2005), 106–17.

24. Citizens petition, 30 Dec. 1831, FC, LP; Eva Sheppard Wolf, *Race and Liberty in the New Nation: Emancipation in Virginia from the Revolution to Nat Turner's Rebellion* (Baton Rouge: Louisiana State University Press, 2006), 244–46; P. J. Staudenraus, *The African Colonization Movement, 1816–1865* (New York: Columbia University Press, 1961). Some American Colonization Society members worried that raising the issue of a constitutional amendment would hurt more than help their cause. See Wolf, *Race and Liberty*, 176.

25. Citizens petitions of 7 Dec., 28 Dec., and 30 Dec. 1831, FC, LP. I am grateful to Michael Caires, who transcribed the names on all of Johnson's petitions and on the Fauquier County petitions of 1830–31. For Moore as counsel to slaves, see, for example, examination of Emanuel, 11 June 1816, FCMB; trial of Randolph, 25 July 1816, ibid.; and *Commonwealth v. Ryal*, 25 Oct. 1819, ibid.

26. Citizens petition, 20 Feb. 1832, FC, LP. Although this petition did not arrive in Richmond until February, it is likely that its subject was part of the public discussions of December.

27. Wolf, *Race and Liberty*, 198–206, 242–43.

28. Memorial of the Ladies of Augusta (three identical copies), 19 Jan. 1832, Augusta Co., LP.

29. Richmond *Enquirer*, 7 and 12 Jan. 1832. Jefferson explained in *Notes on the State of Virginia* (1781–82) that he and the other men in charge of revising Virginia's laws after the Revolution considered, but ultimately withheld, an emancipation scheme. The plan would have freed slaves born after the emancipation act, with the idea that when they reached adulthood they "should be colonized to such place as the circumstances of the time should render most proper." Quotation from p. 264 of the online version at http://etext.virginia.edu/toc/modeng/public/JefVirg .html.

30. The debate ended on 25 Jan. 1832 when the House of Delegates adopted a resolution calling legislation on the abolition of slavery "inexpedient." *Journal of the House of Delegates* (begun Dec. 1831), 109–10; Richmond *Enquirer*, 28 Jan. 1832.

31. John Chandler speech, 17 Jan. 1832, in Richmond *Enquirer*, 24 Feb. 1832 (also at http://etext.lib.virginia.edu/toc/modeng/public/ChaSpee .html); Samuel Moore speech, 11 Jan. 1832, in Richmond *Enquirer*, 19 Jan.

1832; George Summers speech, 17 Jan. 1832, in Richmond *Enquirer*, 14 Feb. 1832. Chandler was from Norfolk County, Moore from Rockbridge County, and Summers from Kanawha County (now in West Virginia).

32. Alexander Knox speech, 17 Jan. 1832, in Richmond *Enquirer*, 11 Feb. 1832; Wolf, *Race and Liberty*, 222–25.

33. *The Speech of Thomas Marshall . . . on the Policy of the State with Respect to Its Colored Population, Delivered January 14, 1832*, 2nd ed. (Richmond: Thomas W. White, 1832), 5, 10.

34. Thomas Marshall speech, 6 Feb. 1832, in Richmond *Enquirer*, 14 Feb. 1832; Wolf, *Race and Liberty*, 232.

35. Citizens testimonial, SJP 1811.

36. SJP 1835; Lucy Malvin petition, 3 Jan. 1838, FC, LP.

37. James Brewer Stewart, *Holy Warriors: The Abolitionists and American Slavery*, rev. ed. (New York: Hill and Wang, 1996), chs. 2–3; Newman, *Transformation of American Abolitionism*, chs. 4–5, quotation from the *Liberator* on p. 129.

38. SJP 1835; RCV 1833, ch. 187.

39. Wolf, *Race and Liberty*, 231–33.

40. RCV 1833, chs. 186, 187.

41. It is possible that they were not twins; one could have been born in January and one in December of that year, but that seems unlikely. The year of their birth comes from the 1880 Census, Washington, D.C. (for Thomas Thornton Withers) and 1870 Census, Washington, D.C. (for Rebecca).

42. Lucy Malvin petition, 3 Jan. 1838, FC, LP.

CHAPTER FIVE. *Race, Identity, and Community*

1. John L. Fant certificate, 9 Jan. 1835, in SJP 1835.

2. RCV 1833, ch. 184, sec. 1.

3. Estimate of the distance from Warrenton to the Pennsylvania line (by road) is from Google Maps. It is about 190 miles by road from Warrenton to Philadelphia.

4. *Johnson v. Malvin*, FN/S1 1833-004, FC Clerk's Loose Papers, FC Circuit Court Records Room, Warrenton.

5. Ibid.

6. Ibid.

7. SJP 1835.

8. Ibid. Phillips signed Johnson's 1824, 1826, and 1827 petitions.

9. They were John A. Cash, Calvin O. Church, William H. Gaines, Joseph Horner, Thomas P. Knox, Joseph Meggine, Thomas L. Moore, Dandall Smith, and William W. Wallace.

10. My rather unscientific survey of petitions to remain in Virginia suggests after about 1820 a trend away from granting such requests. See ch. 1, n. 50, above.

11. The number of women subscribers is around seventy-seven, but it is hard to be sure as some names are difficult to read. For more on women as petitioners, see Elizabeth R. Varon, *We Mean to Be Counted: White Women and Politics in Antebellum Virginia* (Chapel Hill: University of North Carolina Press, 1998), esp. chs. 1–2; and Anne M. Boylan, *The Origins of Women's Activism: New York and Boston, 1797–1840* (Chapel Hill: University of North Carolina Press, 2002), 158–61.

12. Joshua D. Rothman, *Notorious in the Neighborhood: Sex and Families across the Color Line in Virginia, 1787–1861* (Chapel Hill: University of North Carolina Press, 2003), 204–5, 210–12, 233–34, 218–19, 227–31.

13. John Scott to D. C. Brigg, Esqr, 9 Jan. 1834 [1835], in SJP 1835; Ann Norris note, 10 Jan. 1835, ibid.

14. John Scott to D. C. Brigg, Esqr, 9 Jan. 1834 [1835], in SJP 1835.

15. The earliest reference I have come across to the term "white negroes" is a 1786 description of "white negroes, whose skin is altogether of a dead white colour, and whose woolly white hair and features resemble those of their negro parents." John Morgan, "Some Account of a Motley Coloured, or Pye Negro Girl and Mulatto Boy, Exhibited before the Society in the Month of May, 1784, for Their Examination, by Dr. John Morgan, from the History Given of Them by Their Owner Mons. Le Vallois, Dentist of the King of France at Guadaloupe in the West Indies," *Transactions of the American Philosophical Society* 2 (1786): 393. In the twentieth century, some mixed-race people in Mississippi were known as "white negroes," as described in Victoria E. Bynum, "'White Negroes' in Segregated Mississippi: Miscegenation, Racial Identity, and the Law," *Journal of Southern History* 64, no. 2 (May 1998): 247–76. For a discussion of connections between race and traditional views of sun-

darkened workers as inferior, see David Brion Davis, *Inhuman Bondage: The Rise and Fall of Slavery in the New World* (Oxford: Oxford University Press, 2006), 51, 57.

16. Lucy Malvin petition, 3 Jan. 1838, FC, LP; Gary B. Nash, *Forging Freedom: The Formation of Philadelphia's Black Community, 1720–1840* (Cambridge, Mass.: Harvard University Press, 1988).

17. Nash, *Forging Freedom*, 181.

18. SJP 1837.

19. Citizens testimonials, ibid.

20. Samuel Johnson deed of manumission to Lucy Malvin, 18 July 1837, FC Deeds 37:263.

21. CV 1849, Title 30, ch. 107, sec. 2; Lucy Malvin motion, FN/SI Ended Causes 1837-014, FC Clerk's Loose Papers, FC Circuit Court Records Room, Warrenton.

22. Thomas E. Buckley, *The Great Catastrophe of My Life: Divorce in the Old Dominion* (Chapel Hill: University of North Carolina Press, 2002), ch. 1 (quotation on 39). Lucy joined 459 other people who petitioned for absolute divorce between the 1780s and 1840s.

23. Ibid., ch. 1 and appendix.

24. Lucy Malvin petition, 3 Jan. 1838, FC, LP.

25. Ibid.

26. Endorsement, Lucy Malvin petition, 3 Jan. 1838, FC, LP.

27. Charles Irons, *The Origins of Proslavery Christianity: White and Black Evangelicals in Colonial and Antebellum Virginia* (Chapel Hill: University of North Carolina Press, 2008), 12, chs. 3–5, esp. 136.

28. Sandy Elkins's account, FN/SI Ended Causes 1852-013, FC Clerk's Loose Papers, FC Circuit Court Records Room, Warrenton; RFN, entry 605; 1860 Census, Washington, D.C.

29. Lucy Malvin petition, 3 Jan. 1838, FC, LP.

30. Thomas T. Withers will, 2 Jan. 1865, FC Wills 29; estate sale of Thomas T. Withers, entered 29 Mar. 1865, FC Wills 29. The will also freed his servant, Major.

31. Estate sale of Thomas T. Withers, entered 29 Mar. 1865, FC Wills 29. I have read hundreds of wills of emancipation, and only a couple come anywhere near making such provisions. See Eva Sheppard Wolf,

Race and Liberty in the New Nation: Emancipation in Virginia from the Revolution to Nat Turner's Rebellion (Baton Rouge: Louisiana State University Press, 2006), ch. 2.

32. See ch. 2, above.

33. *Commonwealth v. Hughes*, FN/S1 Ended Causes 1849-019, FC Clerk's Loose Papers, photocopy at AAHAFC.

CHAPTER SIX. *Legacies*

1. 1840 Census, Warrenton. In the Johnson household in 1840 were seven people: one free colored man and woman, each aged 55–100 (Samuel and Patty); a free colored woman 24–36 (Lucy); and four free colored children, a boy under 10 (Thornton), a boy aged 10–24 (Samuel Malvin), and two girls under 10 (Becky and probably baby Edinborough).

2. Inventory and appraisement of Samuel Johnson's estate, 31 Jan. 1843, FC Wills 18:115.

3. Samuel Johnson will, 11 Mar. 1836, FC Wills 17:583.

4. *Samuel Johnson v. John Leary*, FC Chancery Court Records, 1838-030, http://www.lva.virginia.gov/chancery/case_detail.asp?CFN=061-1838-030.

5. Ibid.

6. Minute Book, Common Council of the Town of Warrenton, 16 Apr. 1834, Old Jail Museum, Warrenton.

7. *Fant v. Elkins*, 1847-052, http://www.lva.virginia.gov/chancery/case_detail.asp?CFN=061-1847-052, image 6 (Lucy's mark), image 20 (Lucy's signature), image 16 (Samuel Johnson's mark).

8. Samuel Johnson will, 11 Mar. 1836, FC Wills 17:583.

9. Ibid.

10. Samuel Johnson deed to John A. Cash, 6 June 1826, FC Deeds 29:16. John Cash supported Johnson's petitions of 1826, 1828, 1835, and 1837, and also signed the pro-colonization petition of 1831. Since Johnson's purchase of the larger lot is not found in the index to deeds, I am not sure when it took place, but it seems safe to conclude that it was after Johnson sold his well-square parcel to Cash.

11. *Fant v. Elkins*, 1847-052, FC Chancery Court Records, FC Circuit Court Records Room, Warrenton, and http://www.lva.virginia.gov

/chancery/case_detail.asp?CFN=061-1847-052. Johnson did not live in Warrenton as of the late 1830s according to the tax lists: Minute Books, 1834–38, Common Council of the Town of Warrenton, Old Jail Museum, Warrenton.

12. Edinborough's and Jasper's birth years are inferred from later Census records, and also from Samuel Johnson's use of the plural "children" in his codicil.

13. Codicil to Samuel Johnson's will, 10 Aug. 1842, FC Wills 17:583.

14. An account of the debts owed by Johnson's estate suggests that they died around the same time; the estate owed money for two coffins, one that cost fifteen dollars and one that cost twenty dollars. Exhibit (image 24 in the online reproduction), *Fant v. Elkins*.

15. Fant's complaint in *Fant v. Elkins* lists Lucy's children.

16. Bill of complaint, *Fant v. Elkins*.

17. Advertisement and report of sale, *Fant v. Elkins*; John Smith agreement, ibid.

18. Bill of complaint, *Fant v. Elkins*.

19. 1850 Census, Warrenton.

20. Frederick Douglass, *Narrative of the Life of Frederick Douglass, an American Slave*, ed. Deborah E. McDowell (Oxford: Oxford University Press, 1999), 90–91.

21. W. H. Gaines note, receipt, and bill of complaint, *Fant v. Elkins*.

22. Bill of complaint, *Fant v. Elkins*.

23. Charles Bragg deed of manumission to Sandy Elkins, 23 Nov. 1852, FC Deeds 52:98; Sandy Elkins's account, FN/Sl Ended Causes, 1852-013, FC Circuit Court Records Room; RFN, entry 60. In the published transcription of the Register of Free Negroes, Sandy's emancipator is misprinted as Charles Bradford; the microfilm copy of the original shows that Bragg is correct. RFN, microfilm roll 15, LVA.

24. 1860 Census, Washington, D.C., p. 840.

25. Ibid.

26. Ibid., p. 144.

27. 1860 U.S. Census Mortality Schedule, Washington, D.C., found in "U.S. Federal Census Mortality Schedules, 1850–1880," *Ancestry.com*, 2005.

28. Melvin Patrick Ely makes a similar argument in *Israel on the Appomattox: A Southern Experiment in Black Freedom from the 1790s through the Civil War* (New York: Knopf, 2004).

AFTERWORD

1. 1870 Census, Washington, D.C. (Jasper Elkins living with Rebecca Malvin); 1880 Census Washington, D.C., (Jerome Elkins living with William and Edinbara Brown); Boyd's Directory of the District of Columbia, 1894 (Jasper and Jerome Elkins living and working together at 812 3rd St. sw); 1900 Census, Washington, D.C. (Jasper and Jerome Elkins in same household); 1910 Census, Washington, D.C., p. 2B (William H. Browne, Edinborough's son and Jerome's nephew, as a wheelwright).

2. 1930 Census, Cleveland, Ohio (Bertie Cossey, John A. Cossey, Warren Cossey).

3. Waiter: Alpheus Browne, 1910 Census, Atlantic City, N.J.; waitress: Bertie Cossey, 1920 Census, Cleveland, Ohio; fireman: James Brown, 1910 Census, Washington, D.C.; secretary: Bertie Cossey, 1930 Census, Cleveland, Ohio; clerks: Edith Malvin and Josie T. Browne, 1920 Census, Washington, D.C.; seamstress: Josephine (Malvan) Cole, 1910 Census, Washington, D.C.

4. Lawrence Van Gelder, "Show Biz and Romance in the Age of the Cakewalk," *New York Times*, 29 June 1999, accessed online.

5. Nathan Irvin Huggins, *Harlem Renaissance* (Oxford: Oxford University Press, 1971), 280–81; "William C. Elkins," *Internet Broadway Database*, http://www.ibdb.com/person.php?id=34020; 1910, 1920, and 1930 Census, New York City.

6. Tim Brooks, "'Might Take One Disc of This Trash as a Novelty'": Early Recordings by the Fisk Jubilee Singers and the Popularization of 'Negro Folk Music,'" *American Music* 18, no. 3 (Autumn 2000): 278–316.

7. *Crisis* 27, no. 3 (Jan. 1924): 145.

8. Ken Romanowski, liner notes to "Elkins-Payne Jubilee Singers, 1923–29, in Chronological Order," Document Records, Apr. 1995; conversation with Dean Suzuki, San Francisco State University, 18 Nov. 2010;

Robert M. Marovich, "'Glory, Glory to the New Born King': Gospel at Christmastime," *Black Gospel Blog*, http://www.theblackgospelblog .com/2007/12/glory-glory-to-new-born-king-gospel-at.html.

9. Romanowski, liner notes to "Elkins-Payne Jubilee Singers."

10. Garey Browne Jr. obituary, *Washington Post*, 14 Apr. 2000, accessed online.

11. My father recalls black men stepping off the sidewalk to make way for his (white) mother when they visited Washington in the 1950s.

INDEX

RACE IN THE ATLANTIC WORLD, 1700–1900

*The Hanging of Angélique: The Untold Story of
Canadian Slavery and the Burning of Old Montréal*
by AFUA COOPER

*Christian Ritual and the Creation of
British Slave Societies, 1650–1780*
by NICHOLAS M. BEASLEY

*African American Life in the Georgia Lowcountry:
The Atlantic World and the Gullah Geechee*
edited by PHILIP MORGAN

*The Horrible Gift of Freedom: Atlantic Slavery
and the Representation of Emancipation*
by MARCUS WOOD

*The Life and Letters of Philip Quaque,
the First African Anglican Missionary*
edited by VINCENT CARRETTA and TY M. REESE

*In Search of Brightest Africa: Reimagining the
Dark Continent in American Culture, 1884–1936*
by JEANNETTE EILEEN JONES

*Contentious Liberties: American Abolitionists
in Post-emancipation Jamaica, 1834–1866*
by GALE L. KENNY

*We Are the Revolutionists: German-Speaking Immigrants
and American Abolitionists after 1848*
by MISCHA HONECK

The American Dreams of John B. Prentis, Slave Trader
by KARI J. WINTER

*Missing Links: The African and American Worlds
of R. L. Garner, Primate Collector*
by JEREMY RICH

*Almost Free: A Story about Family and Race
in Antebellum Virginia*
by EVA SHEPPARD WOLF